ACTIVITY WORKBOOK

SIDE by SIDE

Plus

3

Steven J. Molinsky • Bill Bliss

with

Carolyn Graham

Contributing Authors

Elizabeth Handley • Dorothy Lynde

Illustrated by

Richard E. Hill

To the Teacher

Side by Side Plus Activity Workbook 3 provides supplemental activities to accompany *Side by Side Plus Student Book 3*. The all-skills activities include listening comprehension practice and GrammarRaps featured on the included Digital Audio CDs. New material in this edition includes activities to support the Student Book Gazette lessons and a new workbook section offering focused practice with life-skill competencies and employment topics. A complete Answer Key enables students to use the Workbook independently for self-study.

(*Side by Side Plus Test Prep Workbook 3*, available separately, offers test preparation practice through achievement tests for all units of the program. The tests are also available as reproducibles included with *Side by Side Plus Teacher's Guide 3*.)

Side by Side Plus Activity Workbook 3

Copyright © 2016 by Pearson Education, Inc.
All rights reserved.

No part of this publication may be reproduced, stored in a retrieval system, or transmitted in any form or by any means, electronic, mechanical, photocopying, recording, or otherwise, without the prior permission of the publisher.

Pearson Education, 10 Bank Street, White Plains, NY 10606

Staff credits: The people who make up the Side by Side Plus team, representing content creation, design, manufacturing, marketing, multimedia, project management, publishing, rights management, and testing are Pietro Alongi, Allen Ascher, Rhea Banker, Elizabeth Barker, Lisa Bayrasli, Elizabeth Carlson, Jennifer Castro, Tracey Munz Cataldo, Diane Cipollone, Aerin Csigay, Victoria Denkus, Dave Dickey, Daniel Dwyer, Wanda España, Oliva Fernandez, Warren Fischbach, Pam Fishman, Nancy Flaggman, Patrice Fraccio, Irene Frankel, Aliza Greenblatt, Lester Holmes, Leslie Johnson, Janet Johnston, Caroline Kasterine, Barry Katzen, Ray Keating, Renee Langan, Jaime Lieber, José Antonio Méndez, Julie Molnar, Alison Pei, Pamela Pia, Stuart Radcliffe, Jennifer Raspiller, Kriston Reinmuth, Mary Perrotta Rich, Robert Ruvo, Tania Saiz-Sousa, Katherine Sullivan, Paula Van Ells, Kenneth Volcjak, Paula Williams, and Wendy Wolf.

Text composition: TSI Graphics, Inc.

Illustrations: Richard E. Hill

The authors gratefully acknowledge the contribution of Tina Carver in the development of the original *Side by Side* program.

ISBN-10: 0-13-418679-6

ISBN-13: 978-0-13-418679-5

Printed in the United States of America

Contents

| what | bake | ⟨cook⟩ | ⟨move⟩ | sit |
| where | compose | ⟨go⟩ | ⟨read⟩ | ⟨watch⟩ |

STUDENT BOOK
PAGES **1–10**

1. A. _____What's_____ Fran _____reading_____?

   B. _____She's reading_____ her e-mail.

2. A. _____Where's_____ Fred _____going_____?

   B. _____he's going_____ to the clinic.

3. A. ___what's___ Nancy ___watching___?

   B. ___She's watching___ a game show.

4. A. ___what's___ you ___cooking___?

   B. ___he's cooking___ dinner.

5. A. ___where are___ you and your wife

   ___maving___?

   B. ___we're moving___ to Miami.

6. A. ___where are___ your grandmother

   and grandfather ___sitting___?

   B. ___they are sitting___ in the park.

7. A. ___what's___ Victor ___composing___?

   B. ___he's composing___ a symphony.

8. A. ___what is___ you ___baking___?

   B. ___I'm baking___ an apple pie.

1.

A. Hi. What ____are____ you doing?

B. ____I'm watching____ a movie on TV.

A. Oh. I don't want to disturb you. __is__ Anna busy?

B. Yes, __she's__. __Taking__ a bath.

A. I'll call back later.

2.

A. Hi, Bill. __are__ the children okay?

B. Yes. __they're__ fine.

A. What __are they__ doing?

B. Vicky __is doing__ her homework, and Timmy __is playing__ baseball in the yard.

A. How about you? __what are you__ doing?

✳ B. __I'm making__ dinner for you and the kids.

A. I'll be home soon.

3.

A. Hello, Peter. This is Mr. Taylor. __is__ your father at home?

B. No, __he isn't__. __he is__ at the health club.

A. Can I speak to your mother?

B. I'm sorry. __she's__ busy right now. __shew__ the washing machine. It's broken.

A. Okay. I'll call back later.

4.

A. Hello, ... Can I speak to ....?

B. I'm sorry. ....

A. Well, can I speak to ....?

B. I'm afraid ....

A. Okay. I'll call back later.

1. *(clean)* I never ____clean____ my apartment, but ____I'm cleaning____ it today

    because __my grandmother is going to visit me__ *(or)* __my boss is coming over for dinner__ .

2. *(iron)* Roger never __iron__ his shirts, but __he's ironing__ them today

    because __he's going to work Tomorrow__ .

3. *(argue)* We never _____ with our landlord, but _____ with him today

    because ....

4. *(worry)* I never _____ about anything, but _____ today because

    ....

5. *(watch)* Betty never _____ the news, but _____ it today because

    ....

6. *(write)* Uncle Phil never _____ to us, but _____ to us today

    because ....

7. *(take)* I never _____ the bus, but _____ it today because

    ....

8. *(comb)* My son never _____ his hair, but _____ it today

    because ....

9. *(get up)* My daughter never _____ early, but _____ early today

    because ....

10. *(smile)* Mr. Grimes never _____, but _____ today because

    ....

11. *(bark)* Our dogs never _____, but _____ today

    because ....

12. *(wear)* Alice never _____ perfume, but _____ it today

    because ....

1. I recommend the fish.

   <u>Do you recommend</u> the chicken, too?

2. My husband bakes delicious cakes. _____ does _____ he _____ bakes _____ pies, too?

3. My daughter gets up early. ⚹_____ dooo _____ your son _____ gets up _____ early, too?

4. They always complain about the traffic. _____ do _____ they _____ complain _____ about the weather, too?

5. Maria speaks Italian and Spanish. _____ does _____ she _____ speaks _____ French, too?

6. My grandson lives in Miami. ⚹_____ doe _____ your granddaughter _____ live _____ there, too?

7. I watch the news every morning. _____ do you watch the news _____ every evening, too?

8. My sister plays soccer. ⚹_____ does your sister play _____ tennis, too?

9. Robert practices the trombone at night. _____ does Robert practices the trombone _____ during the day, too?

10. We plant vegetables every year. _____ do you plant _____ flowers, too?

11. Stanley always adds salt to the stew. _____ does stanley adds _____ pepper, too?

12. I always wear a jacket to work. _____ do you wear _____ a tie, too?

13. My cousin Sue rides a motorcycle. _____ does your cousin rides _____ a bicycle, too?

14. My grandfather jogs every day. _____ does your grandfather jogs _____ when it rains?

15. We need bread from the supermarket. _____ do you need _____ milk, too?

16. Gregory always irons his shirts. _____ does gregory's always irons _____ his pants, too?

17. Our neighbors have three dogs.

    _____ any cats?

Across

3. I like to cook. I'm an excellent ___COOK___.
4. I can type. I'm a very good ___TYPIST___
5. Sally swims fast. She's a fast ___swimmer___.
6. Jeff likes to play sports. He's a good ___athlete___
7. My sons drive taxis. They're both taxi ___drivers___

Down

1. You ski well. You're a very good ___skiier___.
2. We act in plays and movies. We're ___actors___
5. My children love to skate. They're wonderful _____.

F **WHAT'S THE ANSWER?**

Circle the correct answer.

1. Does Hector like to play tennis?
   a. Yes, he likes.
   b. Yes, he does.
   c. Yes, he is.

2. Are you a graceful dancer?
   a. No, I don't.
   b. No, you aren't.
   c. No, I'm not.

3. Does your boss work hard?
   a. Yes, he is.
   b. Yes, he does.
   c. Yes, he works.

4. Is the food at this restaurant spicy?
   a. Yes, it isn't.
   b. Yes, it does.
   c. Yes, it is.

5. Are your children good athletes?
   a. Yes, I am.
   b. Yes, they are.
   c. Yes, they do.

6. Do you and your girlfriend like to cook?
   a. Yes, she does.
   b. Yes, they do.
   c. Yes, we do.

7. Am I a good teacher?
   a. Yes, you are.
   b. Yes, he is.
   c. Yes, you do.

8. Does your husband send e-mail messages to you?
   a. Yes, he is.
   b. Yes, he does.
   c. Yes, she does.

G WHAT ARE THEY SAYING?

1. A. I _____don't_____ like to eat at Albert's house because he ___doesn't___ cook very well.

   B. I know. Everybody says he _isn't_ a very good _cook_. ✱

2. A. I know you _would_ (don't) like to drive with me because you think _I am_ a terrible driver.

   B. That's not true. I think you _drive_ very carefully!

3. A. _do you_ like to type?

   B. No, I _don't_. _I am_ not a very accurate typist.

   A. I disagree. _you are_ an accurate typist, but you _type_ very slowly.

4. A. Oliver Jones is an excellent composer.

   B. I agree. He _composes_ beautifully. I think _he is_ very talented.

5. A. Irene _is not_ going swimming with us today because she _____ like to swim when it's cold.

   B. That's too bad. I really like to go swimming with her. She's a very good _swimmer_.

6. A. I'm jealous of my classmates. They speak English very well, and I _don't_ ✱.

   B. That's not true. Your classmates _speak_ English clearly, but you're a good English _speaker_, too.

H LISTENING

Listen to each question and then complete the answer.

1. Yes, _____he does_____.
2. No, _____she isn't_____.
3. Yes, _they are_ ✓.
4. Yes, _they do_ ✓.
5. No, _she doesn't_ ✓.

6. Yes, _it is_ ✓.
7. No, _he isn't_ ✓.
8. Yes, _I do_ ✓.
9. No, _she doesn't_ ✓.
10. Yes, _he is_ ✓.

11. No, _I'm not_ ✓.
12. Yes, _we do_.
13. Yes, _she is_ ✱
14. No, _they aren't_ ✓.
15. No, _we don't_ ✓.

Listen. Then clap and practice.

A.   Does he like   the movies?

B.   No,   he doesn't.   He likes   TV.

A. Does she like   the mountains?

B.   No,   she doesn't.   She likes   the sea.

A.   Do you like to   hike?

B.   No,   I don't.   I like to   dive.

A.   Do they like to   walk?

B.   No,   they don't.   They like to   drive.

A.   Is he studying   music?

B.   No,   he isn't.   He's studying   math.

A.   Is she taking   a shower?

B.   No,   she isn't.   She's taking   a bath.

A.   Are they living   in Brooklyn?

B.   No,   they aren't.   They're living   in Queens.

A.   Are you washing   your shirt?

B.   No,   I'm not.   I'm washing   my jeans.

J WHAT'S THE QUESTION?

1. We're waiting for <u>the bus</u>.

   What are you waiting for?

2. He's thinking about <u>his girlfriend</u>.

   Who is he thinking about?

3. They're ironing <u>their shirts</u>.

   what are they ironing?

4. I'm calling <u>my landlord</u>.

   who are you calling?

5. She's dancing with <u>her father</u>.

   who is she dancing with?

6. He's watching <u>the news</u>.

   what is he watching?

7. They're complaining about <u>the rent</u>.

   what are they complaining about?

8. She's playing baseball with <u>her son</u>.

   who is she playing baseball with?

9. They're visiting <u>their cousins</u>.

   who Are they visiting with?

10. We're looking at <u>the animals in the zoo</u>.

    what are you looking at?

11. I'm writing about <u>my favorite movie</u>.

    what are you writing about?

12. He's arguing with <u>his boss</u>.

    who is he arguing with?

13. She's knitting a sweater for <u>her daughter</u>.

    who is She knitting a sweater for?

14. We're making <u>pancakes</u>.

    what are you making?

15. I'm sending an e-mail to <u>my uncle</u>.

    who are you sending an email to?

16. They're worrying about <u>their examination</u>.

    what are they worrying about?

17. She's talking to <u>the soccer coach</u>.

    who is she Talking to?

18. He's skating with <u>his grandparents</u>.

    who is he Skating with?

K WHAT ARE THEY SAYING?

1. A. Where are you and your husband taking ___your___ children?

   B. __We're__ taking ___them___ to the zoo.

2. A. Why is Richard calling all ___his___ friends today?

   B. ___he___ wants to tell ___us___ about ___his___ new car.

3. A. What are your parents going to give you for your birthday?

   B. I'm not sure, but ___they___ might give ___me___ a puppy.

4. A. Why is Susie visiting ___her___ grandparents?

   B. ___She___ wants to show ___them___ her new bicycle.

5. A. Why are you wearing a safety helmet on ___yar___ head?

   B. ___I___ don't want to hurt ___my___ head while I'm skateboarding.

6. A. Where are you taking ___your___ new girlfriend on Saturday night?

   B. ___I'm___ taking ___her___ to see the new science fiction movie downtown.

7. A. Why are those students complaining about their teacher?

   B. ___thay___ think she gives ___them___ too much homework.

8. A. Can I tell you and Dad about the party now?

   B. No. We're sleeping now. You can tell ___them___ about ___it___ tomorrow morning.

9. A. Why is Mrs. Jenkins waiting for the plumber?

   B. The sink is leaking. Charlie, the plumber, says ___he___ can fix ___it___.

10. A. Timmy, why are you arguing with ___your___ sister?

    B. ___she___ wants to play with ___my___ new toys, but she can't. They're mine.

1. You should never argue at / **to** / (with) a police officer.

2. We're watching at / to / (—) a game show on TV.

3. You shouldn't shout (at) / to / — people.

4. Do you write at / (to) / from your friends very often?

5. They always complain at / (about) the weather.

6. We visit at / to / (—) our sister's friends in Texas once a year.

7. I'm helping (at) / to / — my neighbors to / (with) / — their garden.

8. I'm always frustrated when I have to wait (for) / — / at the bus.

9. Call to / (—) / at the exterminator right away!

Herbert *(have)* ___had___ 1 a very bad day yesterday. He usually gets up early, but yesterday

morning he *(get up)* ___got up___ 2 very late! He *(eat)* ___ate___ 3 breakfast quickly,

(rush) ___rushed___ 4 out of the house, and *(run)* ___ran___ 5 to the bus stop. Unfortunately, he

(miss) ___missed___ 6 the bus. He *(wait)* ___waited___ 7 for ten minutes, but there weren't

any more buses, so he *(decide)* ___decided___ 8 to walk to his office. Herbert was upset. He

(arrive) ___arrived___ 9 at work two and a half hours late!

Herbert *(sit)* ___sat___ 10 down at his desk and *(begin)* ___began___ 11 his work. He

(call) ___called___ 12 a few people on the telephone, and he *(type)* ___typed___ 13 a few letters.

But he was in a hurry, and he *(make)* ___made___ 14 a lot of mistakes. He *(fix)* ___fixed___ 15

the mistakes, but when he *(finish)* ___finished___ 16 the letters and *(put)* ___put___ 17 them on

his desk, he *(spill)* ___spilled___ 18 water all over them.

At noon, Herbert *(go)* ___went___ 19 to the company cafeteria and *(order)* ___ordered___ 20 a

pizza for lunch. That was a big mistake. The pizza was very spicy, and Herbert *(feel)* ___felt___ 21

sick for the rest of the day.

Herbert's afternoon was even worse than his morning. He *(forget)* ___forgot___ 22 about an

important meeting, his computer *(crash)* ___crashed___ 23, he *(fall)* ___fell___ 24 asleep at his

desk, his chair *(break)* ___broke___ 25, and he *(hurt)* ___hurt___ 26 his arm.

Herbert *(leave)* ___left___ 27 the office at 5:00, *(take)* ___took___ 28 the bus home, and

immediately *(go)* ___went___ 29 to bed! What a terrible, terrible day!

B LISTENING 🔊

Listen and circle the correct answer.

1. yesterday / ~~every day~~ *(every day circled)*
2. ~~yesterday~~ / every day *(yesterday circled)*
3. yesterday / every day
4. yesterday / every day
5. yesterday / every day
6. yesterday / every day
7. yesterday / every day
8. yesterday / every day
9. yesterday / every day
10. yesterday / every day
11. yesterday / every day
12. yesterday / every day

C WHAT'S THE WORD?

Esfuerzo para levantar.

Fill in the missing words. Then read the story aloud.

> decide   lift   need   paint   plant   roller-blade   wait   want

Last Saturday everyone __wanted__ 1 my help. In the morning, I __lifted__ 2 heavy furniture for my wife, and I __painted__ 3 the bathroom walls. Then I __roller bladed__ 4 in the park with my son and __planted__ 5 flowers with my daughter. In the afternoon, my brother __needed__ 6 my help. I went to a store with him and __waited__ 7 while he __decided__ 8 which suit to buy for his wedding.

D PUZZLE: *What Did They Do?*

Across

2. ride
3. teach
5. are
6. meet
7. deliver

Down

1. write
4. get
5. work

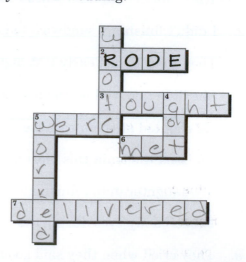

(Crossword answers: 2. RODE, 3. TOUGHT, 5. WERC, 6. MET, 7. DELIVERED, 1 down WROVKD, 4 down GOT, 5 down WOVKD)

WHAT'S THE QUESTION?

1. _____*Did you buy*_____ the green one?   No, I didn't. I bought the blue one.

2. _____ a plane?   No, they didn't. They took a boat.

3. _____ a movie?   No, she didn't. She saw a play.

4. _____ French?   No, he didn't. He spoke Arabic.

5. _____ your arm?   No, I didn't. I broke my leg.

6. _____ at seven?   No, it didn't. It began at eight.

7. _____ to Paris?   No, she didn't. She flew to Rome.

8. _____ the beef?   No, we didn't. We had the chicken.

9. _____ with you?   No, they didn't. They went alone.

10. _____ too softly?   No, you didn't. You sang too loudly.

11. _____ your mother?   No, he didn't. He met my father.

12. _____ your keys?   No, I didn't. I lost my ring.

F **WHAT'S THE ANSWER?**

was	were
wasn't	weren't

angry	hungry	prepared	scared	tired
bored	on time	sad	thirsty	

1. The students fell asleep in Professor Winter's class because _____*they were bored*_____.

2. I didn't finish my sandwich today because _____*I wasn't hungry*_____.

3. They went to bed early last night because _____.

4. She didn't do well on the test because _____.

5. He shouted at them because _____.

6. I missed the train this morning because _____.

7. My daughter didn't finish all her milk because _____.

8. I covered my eyes during the movie because _____.

9. They cried when they said good-bye at the airport because _____.

1. Albert usually drives very carefully.

   He _____*didn't drive*_____ carefully yesterday afternoon.

   He _____*drove*_____ much too fast.

2. Alice usually comes home from work early.

   She _____ home early last night.

   She _____ home late.

3. I usually take the bus to work.

   I _____ the bus this morning.

   I _____ the train.

4. We usually go to the movies on Saturday.

   We _____ to the movies last Saturday.

   We _____ to a concert.

5. Carl and Tom usually forget their homework.

   They _____ their homework yesterday.

   They _____ their lunch.

6. Mr. Tyler usually wears a suit to the office.

   He _____ a suit today.

   He _____ jeans.

7. Professor Hall usually teaches biology.

   She _____ biology last semester.

   She _____ astronomy.

8. Mr. and Mrs. Miller usually eat dinner at 7:00.

   They _____ dinner at 7:00 last night.

   They _____ at 9:00.

9. My grandmother usually gives me a tie for my birthday.

   She _____ me a tie this year.

   She _____ me a watch.

10. Alan usually sits by himself in English class.

    He _____ by himself today.

    He _____ with all his friends.

11. I usually have cereal for breakfast.

    I _____ cereal this morning.

    I _____ eggs.

12. Amanda usually sings very beautifully.

    She _____ beautifully last night.

    She _____ very badly.

1. A. _____*Did you*_____ clean your apartment this week?

   B. No, I ___*didn't*___. I ___*was*___ too lazy.

2. A. _____ meet the company president at the office party?

   B. No, we _____. But we

   _____ his wife.

3. A. _____ Richard fall?

   B. Yes, he _____. He skated

   very quickly, and he _____ very careful.

4. A. _____ Rita deliver all the pizzas today?

   B. No, _____. The people at

   10 Main Street _____ home.

5. A. _____ Roger _____ asleep at the meeting this morning?

   B. No, _____. But he

   _____ asleep later in his

   office. He _____ very tired.

6. A. _____ you ride your motorcycle to work today?

   B. No, _____. I _____

   my bicycle, and I _____ late.

   My supervisor _____ upset.

7. A. _____ like the movie?

B. Yes, I _____. It _____ great! How about you? Did you like it?

A. No, I _____. I thought it _____ boring.

8. A. _____ Mrs. Sanchez your Spanish teacher last semester?

B. Yes, she _____. _____ you in her class?

A. No, _____. I _____ take Spanish. I took French.

9. A. _____ you complain to your landlord about the problems in your apartment?

B. Yes, we _____. He listened to us, but he _____ fix anything. We _____ very angry.

10. A. _____ the students dance gracefully in the school play?

B. No, _____. They _____ very awkwardly. They _____ very nervous.

11. A. Dad, _____ you buy anything at the supermarket?

B. Yes, _____. I _____ some food for dinner.

A. _____ buy any ice cream?

B. Sorry. I _____. There _____ any.

12. A. Grandpa, _____ you a good soccer player when you _____ young?

B. Yes, _____. I _____ a very good player. I _____ fast, and I _____ clumsy.

I HOW DID IT HAPPEN?

1. How did Steven sprain his ankle? *(play tennis)*

   ___He sprained his ankle while he was playing tennis.___

2. How did your sister rip her pants? *(exercise)*

   _____

3. How did you break your arm? *(play volleyball)*

   _____

4. How did James poke himself in the eye? *(fix his sink)*

   _____

5. How did you and your brother hurt yourselves? *(skateboard)*

   _____

6. How did Mr. and Mrs. Davis trip and fall? *(dance)*

   _____

7. How did your father burn himself? *(cook french fries)*

   _____

8. How did your daughter get a black eye? *(fight with the kid across the street)*

   _____

9. How did you cut yourself? *(chop carrots)*

   _____

10. How did Robert lose his cell phone? *(jog in the park)*

    _____

11. How did you _____?

    _____

J GRAMMARRAP: *What Did He Do?*

Listen. Then clap and practice.

A.   What did he   do?

B.   He did   his homework.

A.   What did she   sing?

B.   She sang   a song.

A.   What did they   hide?

B.   They hid   their money.

A.   Where did you   go?

B.   I went to   Hong Kong.

A.   What did he   lose?

B.   He lost his   watch.

A.   What did he   study?

B.   He studied   French.

A.   What did it   cost?

B.   It cost   a lot.

A.   What did they   buy?

B.   They bought   a wrench.

K GRAMMARRAP: *I Was Talking to Bob When I Ran Into Sue*

Listen. Then clap and practice.

I was talking to   Bob when   I ran into   Sue.

I was waiting for   Jack when   I saw   Mary Lou.

They were cleaning   the house when   I knocked on   the door.

He was dusting   a lamp when   it fell   on the floor.

She was learning to   drive when   I met her   last May.

She was buying   a car when   I saw her   today.

WHAT'S THE QUESTION?

How	What	Where
How long	What kind of	Who
How many	When	Why

1. _____ *Who did you meet?* _____   I met <u>the president</u>.

2. _____   She lost <u>her purse</u>.

3. _____   We did our exercises <u>at the beach</u>.

4. _____   They left <u>at 9:15</u>.

5. _____   She got here <u>by plane</u>.

6. _____   He sang <u>in a concert hall</u>.

7. _____   They stayed <u>for a week</u>.

8. _____   I saw a <u>science fiction</u> movie.

9. _____   He cried <u>because the movie was sad</u>.

10. _____   She wrote a letter to <u>her brother</u>.

11. _____   They complained about <u>the telephone bill</u>.

12. _____   We ate <u>a lot of</u> grapes.

13. _____   He spoke <u>at the meeting</u>.

14. _____   They lifted weights <u>all morning</u>.

15. _____   She gave a present to <u>her cousin</u>.

16. _____   I ordered <u>apple</u> pie.

17. _____   We rented <u>seven</u> movies.

18. _____   They sent an e-mail to <u>their teacher</u>.

19. _____   He fell asleep <u>during the lecture</u>.

20. _____   I lost my hat <u>while I was skiing</u>.

1. A. Did you go to Hong Kong?

   B. No, _____we didn't_____.

   A. Where _____did you go_____?

   B. _____We went_____ to Tokyo.

2. A. Did you get there by boat?

   B. No, _____.

   A. How _____?

   B. _____.

3. A. Did your flight to Japan leave on time?

   B. No, _____.

   A. How late _____

   _____?

   B. _____ two hours late.

4. A. Did you have good weather during the flight?

   B. No, _____.

   A. What kind of _____

   _____?

   B. _____ terrible weather.

5. A. Did you stay in a big hotel?

   B. No, _____.

   A. What kind of _____

   _____?

   B. _____.

6. A. Did you eat American food?

   B. No, _____.

   A. What kind of _____

   _____?

   B. _____.

(continued)

7. A. Did you take your camera with you?

    B. No, _____.

    A. What _____

    _____?

    B. _____ our camcorder.

8. A. Did you get around the city by train?

    B. No, _____.

    A. How _____

    _____?

    B. _____.

9. A. Did you meet many Japanese?

    B. No, _____.

    A. Who _____?

    B. _____ other tourists.

10. A. Did you buy any clothing?

    B. No, _____.

    A. What _____?

    B. _____ souvenirs.

Where's the train station?

11. A. Did you speak Japanese?

    B. No, _____.

    A. What language _____

    _____?

    B. _____.

12. A. Did you spend a lot of money?

    B. Yes, _____.

    A. How much _____

    _____?

    B. _____.

SOUND IT OUT! 🔊

Listen to each word and then say it.

this					

1. chicken   3. river   5. busy
2. middle   4. kid   6. didn't

these					

1. cheese   3. asleep   5. Steve
2. meat   4. receive   6. repeat

Listen and put a circle around the word that has the same sound.

1. clean: fine   middle   (these)

2. mix: ski   did   need

3. easy: Rita   break   eyes

4. video: machine   big   keep

5. east: build   little   green

6. symphony: mittens   life   retire

7. rip: knee   maybe   knit

Now make a sentence using all the words you circled, and read the sentence aloud.

8. ....

....

9. meat: Greek   Internet   eight

10. spill: healthy   his   rainy

11. promise: child   key   Richard

12. tea: every   men   into

13. cookie: with   speaks   bricks

14. milk: mine   advice   with

15. team: is   week   attractive

16. typical: sister   lazy   rebuild

Now make a sentence using all the words you circled, and read the sentence aloud.

17. ....

....

WHAT ARE THEY SAYING?

STUDENT BOOK
PAGES 21–32

1. A. Did you ride your bicycle to work this morning?

   B. ___No, I didn't___ . I ___rode___ my

   motorcycle. ___I'm going to ride___ my bicycle to work tomorrow morning.

2. A. Did Tommy wear his new shoes to school today?

   B. _____. He _____

   his old shoes. _____ his new shoes tomorrow.

3. A. Did Sally give her husband a sweater for his birthday this year?

   B. _____. She _____

   him a tie. _____ him a sweater next year.

4. A. Did your parents drive to the mountains last weekend?

   B. _____. They _____ to

   the beach. _____ to the mountains next weekend.

5. A. Did you and your family have eggs for breakfast this morning?

   B. _____. We _____

   pancakes. _____ eggs tomorrow morning.

6. A. Did you go out with Mandy last Saturday night?

   B. _____. I _____

   out with Sandy. _____ out with Mandy next Saturday night.

7. A. Did Howard write an interesting story for homework today?

   B. _____. He _____ a

   boring one. _____ a more interesting story next time.

8. A. Did Shirley leave the office early this afternoon?

   B. _____. She _____

   very late. _____ early tomorrow afternoon.

24 **Activity Workbook**

BAD CONNECTIONS!

1. I'm really scared. Tomorrow my dentist is going to ##########.

   I'm sorry. I can't hear you. I think we have a bad connection. What's ___your dentist going to do___?

2. We're very excited about our trip. We're going to go to ###########.

   What did you say? I can't hear you. Where _____ _____?

3. My son is very sad. His girlfriend is going to move to Alaska because #############.

   I'm sorry. We have a bad connection. Why _____ _____?

4. My parents are going to give me a ########### for my sixteenth birthday.

   Excuse me. I can't hear you. _____ _____?

5. I'm really nervous. I'm going to ########### for the first time tomorrow.

   We have a bad connection. _____ _____?

6. Please come to our wedding. We're going to get married next ###########.

   I'm sorry. I can't hear you. _____ _____?

7. I won't be home after school today. I'm going to meet ###########.

   This is a terrible connection! _____ _____?

(continued)

C LISTENING

Listen and choose the time of the action.

1. a. last night
    b. tomorrow night *(circled)*

2. a. yesterday afternoon
    b. tomorrow afternoon

3. a. this weekend
    b. last weekend

4. a. this Saturday
    b. last Saturday

5. a. last week
    b. next week

6. a. yesterday evening
    b. this evening

7. a. tomorrow night
    b. last night

8. a. this weekend
    b. last weekend

9. a. this evening
    b. yesterday evening

10. a. last winter
    b. this winter

11. a. tomorrow morning
    b. yesterday morning

12. a. next semester
    b. last semester

James is a pessimist. He always thinks the worst will happen.

All his friends are optimists. They always tell James he shouldn't worry.

1. I'm afraid I _____won't have_____ a good time at the office party tomorrow.

    Yes, ___you will___. ____You'll____ have a wonderful time.

2. I'm sure my son _____will hurt_____ himself in his soccer match today.

    No, ___he won't___. ___He won't___ hurt himself. He's always very careful.

3. I'm afraid my grandmother _____ get out of the hospital soon.

    Yes, _____. _____ get out of the hospital in a few days.

4. I'm afraid my wife _____ upset if I get a very short haircut.

    No, _____. _____ be upset.

5. I'm positive I _____ weight on my new diet.

    Yes, _____. _____ lose a lot of weight.

6. I'm afraid my children _____ my birthday this year.

    No, _____. _____ forget your birthday. They never forget it.

7. I'm afraid my landlord _____ our broken doorbell.

    Yes, _____. _____ fix it as soon as he can.

8. I'm afraid my new neighbors _____ like me.

    Of course _____. _____ you a lot. Everybody likes you.

9. I'm sure _____ catch a cold when we go camping this weekend.

    No, _____. _____ catch a cold, James. You worry too much!

| attend | browse | clean | do | fill out | rain | watch | work out |

1. A. Will Amanda be busy this afternoon?

   B. Yes, ____she will____.

   ____She'll be doing____ research at the library.

2. A. Will you be busy this evening?

   B. Yes, _____. _____

   _____ my income tax form.

3. A. Will Donald be home this afternoon?

   B. No, _____. _____

   _____ at his health club.

4. A. Will Mr. and Mrs. Lee be busy tonight?

   B. Yes, _____. _____

   _____ their apartment.

5. A. Will Grandpa be busy tonight?

   B. Yes, _____. _____

   _____ the web until after midnight.

6. A. Will you and your wife be home today?

   B. Yes, _____. _____

   _____ our favorite game show on TV.

7. A. Will Mom be home early tonight?

   B. No, _____. _____

   _____ a meeting.

8. A. Will the weather be nice this weekend?

   B. No, _____. _____

   _____ cats and dogs!

F A TOUR OF MY CITY

Pretend you're taking people on a tour of your city or town. Fill in the blanks with real places you know.

Good morning, everybody. This is .... speaking. I'm so glad you'll be coming with me today on a tour of .... We'll be leaving in just a few minutes.

First, I'll be taking you to see my favorite places in the city: .... , ... , and .... Then we'll be going to .... for lunch. In my opinion, this is the best restaurant in town. After that, I'll be taking you to see the other interesting tourist sights: .... , ... , and .... This evening we'll be going to .... I'm sure you'll have a wonderful time.

G WHAT ARE THEY SAYING?

1. A. I'm sorry. I can't talk right now. I'm
   _____giving_____ the kids a bath.

   B. How much longer _will you be giving_
   them a bath?

2. A. How much longer _____
   _____ your homework?

   B. I'll probably _____
   my homework for another half hour.

   A. Okay. I'll call you then.

3. A. Hi, Carol. This is Bob. Can you
   _____ for a minute?

   B. Sorry. I can't _____ right now.
   I'm _____ for a big test.

4. A. Sorry, Alan. I can't talk now. I'm
   _____ dinner with my family.

   B. How much longer _____
   _____ dinner?

Listen. Then clap and practice.

A.   Will you   be home   at a quarter   to three?

B.   Yes,   I will.   I'll be watching   TV.

A.   Will John   be home   at half   past two?

B.   Yes,   he will.   He'll be cooking   some stew.

A. Will your parents   be home   today   at four?

B.   Yes,   they will.   They'll be washing   the floor.

A.   Will Jane   be home   if I call   at one?

B.   Yes,   she will.   She'll be feeding   her son.

A.   Will you   be home   at half   past eight?

B.   No,   I won't.   I'll be working   late.

A.   Will John   be home   at a quarter   to ten?

B.   No,   he won't.   He'll be visiting   a friend.

A. Will your parents   be home   tonight   at nine?

B.   No,   they won't. They'll be standing   in line.

A.   Will Jane   be home   if I call her   at seven?

B.   No,   she won't.   She'll be dancing   with Kevin.

I WHOSE IS IT?

mine	his	hers	ours	yours	theirs

A. Hi, Robert. I found this wallet in my office today. Is it _____yours_____ [1]?

B. No, it isn't _____ [2], but it might be Tom's.

A. Maybe, but Tom hardly ever visits my office. It probably isn't _____ [3].

B. It's small and blue. Maybe it's Martha's.

A. I asked her this morning. She says it isn't _____ [4].

B. Is there anything inside the wallet?

A. There isn't any money, but there's a picture of three children.

B. It might belong to Mr. Hill. He and his wife have three children.

Maybe the children are _____ [5].

A. I showed the picture to Mr. and Mrs. Hill. They said, "These

children aren't _____ [6]. Our children are older."

B. Maybe you should give the wallet to our supervisor.

A. You know, it might be _____ [7]. She has three children!

B. You're right. I'm positive it's _____ [8]. I saw her children in her office last week.

J GRAMMARRAP: *Where's My Coat?*

Listen. Then clap and practice.

A. Where's   my coat?   I can't find   mine.

Is this one   mine   or yours?

B. That one is   mine.   It isn't   yours.

Yours   is next to   those doors.

A. Where's our umbrella?   We can't find   ours.

Is this one   ours   or theirs?

B. That one is   theirs.   It isn't   yours.

Yours   is under   those chairs.

WHAT DOES IT MEAN?

Circle the correct answer.

1. Jim is wearing a tuxedo today.
   a. He's going to visit his grandmother.
   b. He's going to a wedding.
   c. He's going to work in a factory.

2. My brother has a black eye.
   a. He painted his eye.
   b. He's wearing dark glasses.
   c. He hurt his eye.

3. The teacher wasn't on time.
   a. She was early.
   b. She was late.
   c. She didn't have a good time.

4. They chatted online yesterday.
   a. They used a cell phone.
   b. They used a computer.
   c. They used a fax machine.

5. Everyone in my family is going to relax this weekend.
   a. We're going to rest this weekend.
   b. We're going to retire this weekend.
   c. We're going to return this weekend.

6. He wasn't prepared for his exam.
   a. He didn't study for the exam.
   b. He didn't take the exam.
   c. He was ready for the exam.

7. Could I ask you a favor?
   a. I want to help you.
   b. I want to give you something.
   c. I need your help.

8. It's a very emotional day for Janet.
   a. She's going to work.
   b. She's getting married.
   c. She's studying.

9. He's composing a symphony.
   a. He's writing a symphony.
   b. He's listening to a symphony.
   c. He's going to a concert.

10. George ripped his shirt.
    a. He has to wash his shirt.
    b. He has to iron his shirt.
    c. He has to sew his shirt.

11. Can I borrow your bicycle?
    a. I need your bicycle for a little while.
    b. I want to give you my bicycle.
    c. I want to buy your bicycle.

12. Every day I practice ballet.
    a. I sing every day.
    b. I play violin every day.
    c. I dance every day.

13. I'm going to lend my car to Bob today.
    a. Bob is going to drive my car.
    b. I'm going to drive Bob's car.
    c. Bob is going to give me his car.

14. Mr. and Mrs. Hansen love to talk about their grandchildren.
    a. They listen to them.
    b. They're very proud of them.
    c. They argue with them.

15. Rita did very well on her exam.
    a. She's happy.
    b. She's anxious.
    c. She's sad.

16. I'm going to repair my washing machine.
    a. I'm going to paint it.
    b. I'm going to fix it.
    c. I'm going to do laundry.

17. I need to assemble my new desk.
    a. Can I borrow your screwdriver?
    b. Can I borrow your ladder?
    c. Can I borrow your chair?

18. I sprained my ankle.
    a. I broke my ankle.
    b. I hurt my ankle.
    c. I poked my ankle.

19. I'm going to fill out my income tax form.
   a. I'm going to return it.
   b. I'm going to read it.
   c. I'm going to answer the questions on the form.

20. They're playing Scrabble.
   a. They're playing a game.
   b. They're playing a sport.
   c. They're playing an instrument.

21. Mr. Smith is complaining to his boss.
   a. He's talking about his boss, and he's upset.
   b. He's talking to his boss, and he's happy.
   c. He's talking to his boss, and he's upset.

22. I'm going to call my wife right away.
   a. I'm going to call her immediately.
   b. I'm going to call her in a few hours.
   c. I'm going to call her when I have time.

23. My sister is an excellent athlete.
   a. She's an active person.
   b. She plays sports very well.
   c. She likes to watch sports.

24. My mother is looking forward to her retirement.
   a. She's happy about her new job.
   b. She wants to buy new tires for her car.
   c. Soon she won't have to go to work every day.

L LISTENING: *Looking Forward*

Listen to each story. Then answer the questions.

What Are Mr. and Mrs. Miller Looking Forward to?

1. Mr. and Mrs. Miller _____ last week.
   (a.) moved
   b. relaxed
   c. flew to Los Angeles

2. Mr. and Mrs. Miller aren't going to _____ this weekend.
   a. repaint their living room
   b. assemble their computer
   c. relax in their yard

3. They're going to _____ next weekend.
   a. assemble their computer
   b. relax
   c. paint flowers

What's Jonathan Looking Forward to?

4. Jonathan isn't _____ today.
   a. sitting in his office
   b. thinking about his work
   c. thinking about next weekend

5. Next weekend he'll be _____.
   a. working
   b. cooking and cleaning
   c. getting married

6. On their trip to Hawaii, Jonathan and his wife won't be _____.
   a. swimming in the ocean
   b. paying bills
   c. eating in restaurants

What's Mrs. Grant Looking Forward to?

7. When she retires, Mrs. Grant will be _____.
   a. getting up early
   b. getting up late
   c. taking the bus to work

8. Mrs. Grant will _____ with her friends.
   a. go to museums
   b. work in her garden
   c. read books

9. She'll take her grandchildren to _____.
   a. the park and the beach
   b. the zoo and the beach
   c. the park and the zoo

✔ CHECK-UP TEST: Chapters 1–3

A. Fill in the blanks.

Ex. Ann ___is___ a good skater, and her children ___skate___ well, too.

1. A. Mr. and Mrs. Lee _____ wonderful dancers.

   B. I agree with you. They _____ very well.

2. A. Roger _____ very carelessly.

   B. I know. He's a terrible driver.

3. A. We don't swim very well.

   B. I disagree. I think _____ excellent _____.

4. A. I type very well. I think _____ a very good _____.

5. A. We _____ good _____, but we like to ski anyway.

B. Fill in the blanks.

1. A. Did you speak to Mrs. Baxter yesterday?

   B. No, I _____. I _____ too busy. But I _____ to Mrs. Parker.

2. A. Did you buy juice when you were at the store?

   B. No, I _____. I forgot. But I _____ milk.

3. A. _____ they get up early this morning?

   B. No, they _____. They _____ up very late.

4. A. Did Mr. Wong teach biology last semester?

   B. No, he _____. He _____ astronomy because the astronomy teacher _____ sick all semester.

5. A. _____ you talk to Tom last night?

   B. No, I _____. I _____ to his wife. Tom _____ there when I called.

C. Write the questions.

Ex. We're arguing with <u>our landlord</u>.

   <u>Who are you arguing with?</u>

1. I'm writing about <u>my favorite movie</u>.

   _____

2. They're going to fix <u>their bookcase</u>.

   _____

3. He hiked <u>in the mountains</u>.

   _____

4. She'll be ready <u>in a few minutes</u>.

   _____

5. They arrived <u>by plane</u>.

   _____

6. We'll be staying until <u>Monday</u>.

   _____

7. She's going to hire <u>five</u> people.

   _____

D. Answer the questions.

Ex. What did your daughter do yesterday morning?

(do her homework) _____ She did her homework. _____

1. What's your sister doing today?

(adjust her satellite dish) _____

2. What does your brother do every evening?

(chat online) _____

3. What are you going to do next weekend?

(visit my mother-in-law) _____

4. What did Jack and Rick do yesterday afternoon?

(deliver groceries) _____

5. What was David doing when his children came home from school?

(bake a cake) _____

6. How will you get to work tomorrow?

(take the bus) _____

7. What will you and your husband be doing this evening?

(watch TV) _____

8. How did you cut your hand?

(chop carrots) _____

E. Listen to each question and then complete the answer.

Ex. Yes, _____ he does _____.

1. Yes, _____.

2. No, _____.

3. Yes, _____.

4. Yes, _____.

5. No, _____.

6. Yes, _____.

7. No, _____.

8. Yes, _____.

Read the first article on student book page 33 and answer the questions.

SIDE *by* SIDE *Gazette*

STUDENT BOOK
PAGES **33–36**

1. More than 145 million immigrants ____.
   a. live outside
   b. move to be with family members
   c. live in urban neighborhoods
   d. leave their countries

2. ____ are examples of natural disasters.
   a. Political problems
   b. Bad living conditions
   c. Floods and earthquakes
   d. Wars

3. The main idea of paragraph 1 is immigrants ____.
   a. are everywhere
   b. have economic problems
   c. have political problems
   d. move for many different reasons

4. According to paragraph 2, many immigrants move from ____.
   a. North Africa to Western Europe
   b. Asia to Africa
   c. Latin America to Asia
   d. Western Europe to Eastern Europe

5. ____ has a larger percentage of immigrants than New York.
   a. Los Angeles
   b. Saudi Arabia
   c. Athens
   d. Rome

6. In Saudi Arabia ____ is native born.
   a. 10% of the population
   b. 40% of the population
   c. 50% of the population
   d. 90% of the population

7. The author refers to Esquilino as a *historic* neighborhood because ____.
   a. it's an urban neighborhood
   b. it has many Chinese immigrants
   c. it has a long history
   d. it has many schools that teach history

8. According to this article, in New York ____.
   a. the schools teach 140 languages
   b. 40% of the people were born in a foreign country
   c. 50% of the children are foreign born
   d. there are fewer immigrants than in Los Angeles

9. According to this article, ____.
   a. most immigrants are from Asia
   b. most immigrants live far from the city
   c. immigration changes neighborhoods
   d. most immigrants in Los Angeles are children

10. Immigrants probably move to urban neighborhoods because ____.
    a. urban neighborhoods have many jobs
    b. urban neighborhoods are very clean
    c. urban neighborhoods are expensive
    d. urban neighborhoods are historic

B FACT FILE

Look at the Fact File on student book page 33 and answer the questions.

1. The United States has twenty-four million more immigrants than ____.
   a. Germany
   b. Saudi Arabia
   c. Australia
   d. Canada

2. Canada has 600,000 more immigrants than ____.
   a. Germany
   b. Australia
   c. Saudi Arabia
   d. France

C ELLIS ISLAND

Read the second article on student book page 33 and answer the questions.

1. Ellis Island was an immigration center for ____.
   a. 54 years   c. 92 years
   b. 62 years   d. 100 years

2. Immigrants who came to the United States in ____ stopped at Ellis Island.
   a. 1800   c. 1900
   b. 1850   d. 1955

3. You can infer that immigrants who came to Ellis Island arrived ____.
   a. by plane   c. by bus
   b. by boat   d. by train

4. There weren't many immigrants from ____ at Ellis Island.
   a. Italy   c. Australia
   b. Germany   d. Austria

5. In paragraph 1, a *harbor* refers to ____.
   a. a building
   b. a neighborhood
   c. the ocean
   d. part of a body of water where boats can land

6. At Ellis Island officials DIDN'T ____.
   a. give English examinations
   b. check immigrants' documents
   c. give medical examinations
   d. send some immigrants back to their countries

7. Officials at Ellis Island probably gave medical examinations because ____.
   a. they wanted to help immigrants
   b. they were looking for doctors
   c. they didn't have enough hospitals
   d. they wanted to keep unhealthy people out of the country

D INTERVIEW

Read the interview on student book page 34 and answer the questions.

1. Tran came to Australia because ____.
   a. he wanted to learn English
   b. his wife's family was there
   c. his wife and children were there
   d. his brother's family was there

2. You can infer that Melbourne is ____.
   a. a city in Australia
   b. the capital of Australia
   c. a neighborhood in Australia
   d. a rural area in Australia

3. You know from the interview that ____ in Vietnam.
   a. Tran worked seven days a week
   b. Tran taught mathematics
   c. Tran's brother owned a restaurant
   d. Tran's wife had a good job

4. You can conclude that Tran does not work as ____.
   a. a waiter
   b. an assembler
   c. a cashier
   d. a cook

5. You can infer that Tran is working in a restaurant because ____.
   a. his brother owns the restaurant
   b. he likes to cook
   c. he has experience
   d. he wants to go to college

6. In the last sentence, *grateful* means ____.
   a. excited
   b. sure
   c. thankful
   d. nervous

E WE'VE GOT MAIL! What's the Word?

Choose the words that best complete each sentence.

1. My birthday _____ tomorrow.
   a. will
   b. going to
   c. is
   d. is going to

2. The library _____ at 9 A.M. tomorrow.
   a. opening
   b. open
   c. opened
   d. opens

3. Jared _____ his parents in Miami next month.
   a. going to visit
   b. is visiting
   c. will going to visit
   d. going visiting

4. _____ getting married next June.
   a. We
   b. We'll
   c. We're
   d. We're going

5. Al's Department Store _____ a sale next week.
   a. is having
   b. having
   c. have
   d. will be

6. The bus to Canton _____ at 2:30 P.M.
   a. leaving
   b. leaves
   c. goes to leave
   d. going to leave

7. They _____ to the movies next Saturday.
   a. don't be going
   b. won't going
   c. can't going
   d. aren't going

8. The concert _____ in ten minutes.
   a. will
   b. begins
   c. going
   d. going to

F WE'VE GOT MAIL! What's the Sentence?

Choose the sentence that is correct and complete.

1. a. The train arrived at 3:00 tomorrow.
   b. The train arriving at 3:00 tomorrow.
   c. The train arrives at 3:00 tomorrow.
   d. The train is going arrive at 3:00 tomorrow.

2. a. I'm taking a vacation next June.
   b. I go to take a vacation next June.
   c. I took a vacation next June.
   d. I'll be going to take a vacation next June.

3. a. The play starting at 6:30.
   b. The play will going to start at 6:30.
   c. The play going to start at 6:30.
   d. The play starts at 6:30.

4. a. There be no school tomorrow.
   b. There's no school tomorrow.
   c. There's being no school tomorrow.
   d. There going to be no school tomorrow.

5. a. We doing homework tonight.
   b. We're going to homework tonight.
   c. We're doing homework tonight.
   d. We'll be going to do homework tonight.

6. a. I'm going to skiing this weekend.
   b. I go to skiing this weekend.
   c. I going skiing this weekend.
   d. I'm going skiing this weekend.

G FUN WITH IDIOMS!

Choose the best response.

1. I'll give you a ring tomorrow.
   a. Thanks. You're very generous.
   b. No thanks. I already have one.
   c. Give it to me now!
   d. Good. I'll talk to you then.

2. It's raining cats and dogs!
   a. Did you close all the windows?
   b. I think I'll walk the dog.
   c. Call the landlord and complain.
   d. There are too many pets in this neighborhood.

3. This job is no picnic.
   a. I'm glad you like it.
   b. The food is terrible.
   c. After a while, it will get easier.
   d. Have another piece of cake.

4. I'm tied up right now.
   a. I have a lot of free time, too.
   b. You look great.
   c. Is this a good time to talk?
   d. Sorry. I'll call you back later.

5. What's cooking?
   a. Fine thanks. And you?
   b. Not much.
   c. Are you hungry?
   d. I need a few things at the supermarket.

6. That homework assignment was a piece of cake. Do you agree?
   a. Yes. I finished it in ten minutes.
   b. Yes. I couldn't understand it.
   c. I don't agree. It was very easy.
   d. Yes. I have a stomachache.

H "CAN-DO" REVIEW

Match the "can do" statement and the correct sentence.

_____ 1. I can tell about current activities.

_____ 2. I can tell about past activities.

_____ 3. I can tell about future plans.

_____ 4. I can ask about likes.

_____ 5. I can tell about my goals.

_____ 6. I can describe my feelings and emotions.

_____ 7. I can react to bad news.

_____ 8. I can tell about the time of an event.

_____ 9. I can tell about the duration of an event.

_____ 10. I can ask a favor.

a. I'm going to wear my new jacket tomorrow.

b. I want to be a famous actor.

c. I'll be doing homework for another hour.

d. That's a shame!

e. I'm watching the news.

f. The movie will begin in a few minutes.

g. Do you like to swim?

h. Could you do me a favor?

i. I cleaned my apartment yesterday.

j. I was happy.

STUDENT BOOK PAGES 37–50

1. I ride horses.

   _____I've ridden_____ horses for many years.

2. I fly airplanes.

   _____ airplanes for several years.

3. I give injections at the hospital.

   _____ injections for many years.

4. I speak Italian.

   _____ it all my life.

5. I take photographs.

   _____ them for many years.

6. I do exercises every day.

   _____ them every day for many years.

7. I draw cartoons.

   _____ cartoons for several years.

8. I write for a newspaper.

   _____ for a newspaper for many years.

9. I drive carefully.

   _____ carefully all my life.

B LISTENING

Listen and choose the word you hear.

1. a. ridden
   b. written

2. a. taking
   b. taken

3. a. giving
   b. given

4. a. written
   b. driven

5. a. writing
   b. written

6. a. drawing
   b. doing

7. a. spoken
   b. speaking

8. a. done
   b. drawn

| be | fly | give | ride | sing | take |
| draw | get | go | see | swim | write |

1. _I've never flown_
in a helicopter.

2. _____
a raise.

3. _____
in a limousine.

4. _____
a cartoon.

5. _____
a book.

6. _____
a trip to Hawaii.

7. _____
in a choir.

8. _____
in the Mediterranean.

9. _____
on television.

10. _____
on a cruise.

11. _____
a present to my teacher.

12. _____
a Broadway show.

D LISTENING

Is Speaker B answering *Yes* or *No*? Listen to each conversation and circle the correct answer.

1. (Yes)   No   3. Yes   No   5. Yes   No   7. Yes   No

2. Yes   No   4. Yes   No   6. Yes   No   8. Yes   No

E WHAT ARE THEY SAYING?

fall	get	give	go	ride	wear

1. A. _____Have you ever gotten_____ stuck in bad traffic?

    B. Yes. As a matter of fact, _____I got_____ stuck in very bad traffic this morning.

2. A. _____ on a Ferris wheel?

    B. Yes, I have. _____ on a Ferris wheel last weekend.

3. A. _____ a tuxedo?

    B. Yes, I have. _____ a tuxedo to my sister's wedding.

4. A. _____ scuba diving?

    B. Yes, I have. _____ scuba diving last summer.

5. A. _____ blood?

    B. Yes, I have. _____ blood a few months ago.

6. A. _____ on the sidewalk?

    B. Yes. In fact, _____ on the sidewalk a few days ago.

F GRAMMARRAP: *Have You Ever?*

Listen. Then clap and practice.

A. Have you ever   seen   a rainbow?

    Have you ever   learned   to dance?

    Have you ever   flown   an airplane?

    Have you ever   gone   to France?

B. No, I've never   seen   a rainbow.

    I've never   learned   to dance.

    I've never   flown   an airplane.

    But I've often   gone   to France.

38 Activity Workbook

WHAT ARE THEY SAYING?

drive	eat	go	meet	see	speak	take	write

1. A. ___Have___ your children ___eaten___ breakfast yet?

   B. Yes, ___they have___. ___They ate___ breakfast a little while ago.

2. A. _____ George _____ his new car yet?

   B. Yes, _____. _____ it for the first time this morning.

3. A. _____ Gloria _____ to the post office yet?

   B. Yes, _____. _____ to the post office a little while ago.

4. A. _____ you and Jane _____ the new movie at the Westville Mall?

   B. Yes, _____. _____ it last Saturday night.

5. A. _____ the employees _____ inventory yet?

   B. Yes, _____. _____ inventory last weekend.

6. A. _____ you _____ to the landlord yet?

   B. Yes, _____. _____ to him this morning.

7. A. _____ I _____ a letter to the Carter Company yet?

   B. Yes, _____. _____ them a letter last week.

8. A. _____ you and your wife _____ your daughter's new boyfriend yet?

   B. Yes, _____. _____ him last Friday night.

1. Kenji and his girlfriend aren't going to eat at Burger Town today. ___They've___ already ____eaten____ at Burger Town this week. ___They ate___ there on Monday.

2. My sister isn't going dancing tonight. _____ already _____ dancing this week. _____ dancing last night.

3. Timothy isn't going to wear his new jacket to work today. _____ already _____ it to work this week. _____ it yesterday.

4. My husband and I aren't going to do our laundry today. _____ already _____ our laundry this week. _____ it on Saturday.

5. Roger isn't going to give his girlfriend candy today. _____ already _____ her candy this week. _____ her candy yesterday morning.

6. I'm not going to see a movie today. _____ already _____ a movie this week. _____ a movie on Wednesday.

7. We aren't going to buy fruit at the supermarket today. _____ already _____ fruit at the supermarket this week. _____ some fruit two days ago.

8. Susie isn't going to visit her grandparents today. _____ already _____ them this week. _____ them yesterday.

9. David isn't going to take his children to the circus today. _____ already _____ them to the circus this week. _____ them to the circus a few days ago.

I WHAT'S THE WORD?

go
went
gone

1. We should _____go_____ now.

2. They _____went_____ home early today.

3. She's already _____gone_____ home.

see
saw
seen

4. I've never _____ him.

5. I _____ her yesterday.

6. Do you _____ them often?

eat
ate
eaten

7. I _____ there this morning.

8. Has he ever _____ there?

9. Do you _____ there every day?

write
wrote
written

10. How often do you _____ to them?

11. She's already _____ her report.

12. He _____ her a very long letter.

wear
wore
worn

13. When will you _____ it?

14. He's never _____ it.

15. She _____ it today.

speak
spoke
spoken

16. Who _____ to you about it?

17. She can't _____ Chinese.

18. Have they _____ to you?

drive
drove
driven

19. They've never _____ there.

20. We never like to _____ there.

21. She _____ there today.

do
did
done

22. Did you _____ your homework?

23. We _____ that yesterday.

24. Have you ever _____ that?

1. A. Janet, you've got to do your homework.

   B. But, Mother, _I've_ already _____ my homework today.

   A. Really? When?

   B. Don't you remember? _____ my homework this afternoon.

   A. Oh, that's right. Also, _____ you _____ a letter to Grandma yet?

   B. Yes, _____. I wrote to her yesterday.

2. A. Would you like to swim at the health club tonight?

   B. I don't think so. _____ already _____ at the health club today.

   A. Really? When?

   B. _____ there this morning.

3. A. Are you going to take your vitamins?

   B. _____ already _____ them.

   A. Really? When?

   B. _____ them before breakfast.

   How about you? _____ you _____ yours?

   A. Yes, _____. I _____ mine when I got up.

4. A. I hope Jimmy gets a haircut soon.

   B. Don't worry, Mother. _____ already _____ one.

   A. I'm glad to hear that. When?

   B. _____ a haircut yesterday.

   A. That's wonderful!

5. A. When are you and Fred going to eat at the new restaurant downtown?

B. _____ already _____ there.

A. Really? When?

B. _____ there last weekend.

A. How was the food?

B. It was terrible. It was the worst food we've ever _____!

6. A. When are you going to speak to the boss about a raise?

B. _____ already _____ to her.

A. Really? When?

B. _____ to her this morning.

A. What did she say?

B. She said, "..."

K **GRAMMARRAP:** *Have You Gone to the Bank?*

Listen. Then clap and practice.

A. Have you gone to the   bank?

B.   Yes,   I have.

     I went to the   bank   at noon.

A. Have they taken   a vacation?

B.   Yes,   they have.

     They took   a vacation   in June.

A. Has he written   the letters?

B.   Yes,   he has.

     He wrote   the letters   today.

A. Has she gotten   a raise?

B.   Yes,   she has.

     She got   a raise   last May.

buy	dance	fly	go	read	see	swim
clean	eat	give	make	ride	study	take

1. A. What's the matter, Susan? You aren't riding very well today.

   B. I know. ___I haven't ridden___ in a long time.

2. A. I can't believe it! These cars are very expensive.

   B. Remember, we _____ a new car in a long time.

3. A. Are you nervous?

   B. Yes, I am. _____ in an airplane in a long time.

4. A. Are you excited about your vacation?

   B. Yes, I am. _____ a vacation in a long time.

5. A. You aren't swimming very well today.

   B. I know. _____ in a long time.

6. A. Buster is really hungry.

   B. I know. He _____ anything in a long time.

7. A. Susie's room is very dirty.

   B. I know. She _____ it in a long time.

8. A. I think Timmy watches too much TV.

   B. You're right. _____ a book in a long time.

9. A. Mom, who was the sixteenth president of the United States?

B. I'm not sure. _____ American history in a long time.

10. A. Everyone says the new movie at the Center Cinema is excellent.

B. Let's see it. We _____ a good movie in a long time.

11. A. Are you nervous?

B. Yes, I am. _____ blood in a long time.

12. A. What's Dad doing?

B. He's making dinner. _____ dinner in a long time.

13. A. Is there any fruit in the refrigerator?

B. No, there isn't. I _____ to the supermarket in a long time.

14. A. Ouch!!

B. Sorry. _____ in a long time.

M **PUZZLE:** *What Have They Already Done?*

Across
1. wash
5. fly
8. go
10. explain
11. meet
12. take

Down
2. see
3. drive
4. play
6. wear
7. drink
8. get
9. be

W A S H E D

Richard is going to have a party tonight, and he has a lot of things to do.

✔	go to the supermarket
	clean my apartment
✔	get a haircut
	bake a cake
✔	fix my CD player

1. _____ He's already gone to the supermarket. _____

2. _____ He hasn't cleaned his apartment yet. _____

3. _____

4. _____

5. _____

Susan is going to work this morning, and she has a lot of things to do.

✔	take a shower
	do my exercises
	feed the cat
✔	walk the dog
	eat breakfast

6. _____

7. _____

8. _____

9. _____

10. _____

Beverly and Paul are going on a trip tomorrow, and they have a lot of things to do.

	do our laundry
✔	get our paychecks
✔	pay our bills
	pack our suitcases
	say good-bye to our friends

11. _____

12. _____

13. _____

14. _____

15. _____

Roberta is very busy today.
She has a lot of things to
do at the office.

✔	write to Mrs. Lane
✔	call Mr. Sanchez
☐	meet with Ms. Wong
☐	read my e-mail
✔	send a fax to the Ace Company

16. _____

17. _____

18. _____

19. _____

20. _____

You have a lot of things to do today. What have you done? What haven't you done?

1. ....

2. ....

3. ....

4. ....

5. ....

LISTENING 🔊

What things have these people done? What haven't they done? Listen and check _Yes_ or _No_.

		Yes	No			Yes	No
1.	do homework	✔	____	5.	do the laundry	____	____
	practice the violin	____	✔		vacuum the rugs	____	____
2.	write the report	____	____	6.	get the food	____	____
	send a fax	____	____		clean the house	____	____
3.	feed the dog	____	____	7.	speak to the landlord	____	____
	eat breakfast	____	____		call Ajax Electric	____	____
4.	fix the pipes	____	____	8.	hook up the VCR	____	____
	repair the washing machine	____	____		read the instructions	____	____

1. A. Have you spoken to David recently?

   B. Yes, I ___have___. I _____ to him last night.

   A. What _____ he say?

   B. He's worried because he's going to fly in a helicopter this week, and he's never _____ in a helicopter before.

2. A. _____ you seen any good movies recently?

   B. No, I _____. I _____ a movie last week, but it was terrible.

   A. Really? What movie did you _____?

   B. *The Man from Madagascar.* It's one of the worst movies I've ever _____.

3. A. I think I forgot to do something, but I can't remember what I forgot to do.

   B. Have you _____ the mail to the post office?

   A. Yes. I _____ it to the post office an hour ago.

   B. _____ you _____ a fax to the Ace Company?

   A. Yes. I _____ them a fax this morning.

   B. _____ you _____ the employees their paychecks?

   A. Uh-oh! That's what I forgot to do!

4. A. _____ you gone on vacation yet?

   B. Yes, I _____. I _____ to Venice. It was phenomenal!

   A. _____ you ever _____ to Venice before?

   B. Yes, I _____. I _____ there a few years ago.

5.

A. What _____ you get for your birthday?

B. My family _____ me seventy-five dollars.

A. That's fantastic! What _____?

B. Going to buy? I've already _____ all my birthday money.

A. Really? What _____ buy?

B. I _____ a lot of songs. Do you want to _____ to them?

6.

A. Are you ready to leave soon?

B. No, _____. I haven't _____ a shower yet.

A. But you _____ up an hour ago. You're really slow today. _____ you eaten breakfast yet?

B. Of course _____. I _____ a little while ago, and I've already _____ the dishes.

A. Well, hurry up! It's 8:30. I don't want to be late.

Q LISTENING

Listen to each word and then say it.

j!

1. job
2. jacket
3. juice
4. jam
5. jog
6. pajamas
7. journalist
8. just
9. Jennifer

10. you
11. yoga
12. yellow
13. yard
14. yesterday
15. young
16. yogurt
17. yet
18. New York

y!

R JULIA'S BROKEN KEYBOARD

Julia's keyboard is broken. The j's and the y's don't always work.
Fill in the missing j's and y's and then read Julia's letters aloud.

1.

_J_udy,

   Have you seen my blue and
_y_ellow _j_acket at __our house?
I think I left it there __esterday
after the __azz concert. I've looked
everywhere, and I __ust can't find
it anywhere.

   __ulia

2.

Dear __ennifer,

   We're sorry __ou haven't been able
to visit us this __ear. Do __ou think
__ou could come in __une or __uly?
We really en__oyed __our visit last
__ear. We really want to see __ou
again.

   __ulia

3.

__eff,

   __ack and I have gone out __ogging,
but we'll be back in __ust a few
minutes. Make __ourself comfortable.
__ou can wait for us in the __ard. We
haven't eaten lunch __et. We'll have
some __ogurt and orange __uice when
we get back.

   __ulia

4.

Dear __ane,

   We __ust received the beautiful
pa__amas __ou sent to __immy.
Thank __ou very much. __immy is
too __oung to write to __ou himself,
but he says "Thank __ou." He's
already worn the pa__amas, and
he's en__oying them a lot.

   __ulia

5.

Dear __anet,

   __ack and I are coming to visit
__ou and __ohn in New __ork. We've
been to New __ork before, but we
haven't visited the Statue of Liberty
or the Empire State Building __et.
See __ou in __anuary or maybe in
__une.

   __ulia

6.

Dear __oe,

   We got a letter from __ames last
week. He has en__oyed college a lot
this __ear. His favorite sub__ects
are German and __apanese. He's
looking for a __ob as a __ournalist
in __apan, but he hasn't found one
__et.

   __ulia

1. <u>He's</u> already eaten lunch.

   _____ is

   ✔ has

2. <u>He's</u> eating lunch.

   ✔ is

   _____ has

3. <u>She's</u> taking a bath.

   _____ is

   _____ has

4. <u>She's</u> taken a bath.

   _____ is

   _____ has

5. <u>He's</u> having a good time.

   _____ is

   _____ has

6. <u>She's</u> going to get up.

   _____ is

   _____ has

7. <u>He's</u> bought a lot of music recently.

   _____ is

   _____ has

8. <u>It's</u> snowing.

   _____ is

   _____ has

9. <u>She's</u> thirsty.

   _____ is

   _____ has

10. <u>He's</u> got to leave now.

    _____ is

    _____ has

11. <u>Where's</u> the nearest health club?

    _____ is

    _____ has

12. <u>She's</u> written the report.

    _____ is

    _____ has

13. <u>He's</u> taking a lot of photographs.

    _____ is

    _____ has

14. <u>He's</u> taken a few photographs.

    _____ is

    _____ has

15. <u>He's</u> spent all his money.

    _____ is

    _____ has

16. <u>There's</u> a library across the street.

    _____ is

    _____ has

17. <u>She's</u> gone kayaking.

    _____ is

    _____ has

18. <u>It's</u> very warm.

    _____ is

    _____ has

19. <u>He's</u> embarrassed.

    _____ is

    _____ has

20. This is the best book <u>she's</u> ever read.

    _____ is

    _____ has

for	since

1.

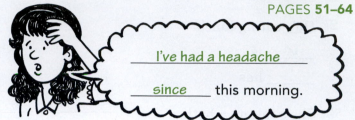

How long have you had a headache?

I've had a headache

since this morning.

2. How long have your parents been married?

_____ a long time.

3. How long has your brother owned a motorcycle?

_____ last summer.

4. How long has your sister been interested in astronomy?

_____ several years.

5. How long have you had a cell phone?

_____ last month.

6. How long have you and your husband known each other?

_____ 1994.

7. How long have the Wilsons had a dog?

_____ a few weeks.

8. How long have you had problems with your upstairs neighbor?

_____ a year.

9. How long has your daughter been a computer programmer?

_____ 2000.

10. How long has your son played in the school orchestra?

_____ September.

11. How long have there been mice in your attic?

_____ two months.

B WHAT'S THE QUESTION?

1. _____How long has_____ your daughter
   _____wanted to be an engineer_____?

   She's wanted to be an engineer for a long time.

2. _____ James
   _____?

   He's owned his own house since 2001.

3. _____ your grandparents
   _____?

   They've been married for 50 years.

4. _____ you
   _____?

   I've been interested in photography since last year.

5. _____ Gregory
   _____?

   He's worn glasses since last spring.

6. _____ your cousins
   _____?

   They've known how to snowboard for a few years.

7. _____ your son
   _____?

   He's had a girlfriend for several months.

8. _____ there
   _____?

   There's been a pizza shop in town since last fall.

Listen. Then clap and practice.

A. How long have you   known   Maria?

B. I've known her   since I was   two.

A. Have you met   her older   sister?

B. No, I haven't.   Have you?

A. How long   has your son   been in college?

B. He's been there   since early   September.

A. Does he like   all of his   courses?

B. I think so.   I can't   remember.

A. How long have   your friends   lived in London?

B. They've lived there   since two thousand   one.

A. Have you visited them   since they   moved there?

B. Yes, I have.   It was fun.

A. How long has   your brother   been married?

B. He's been married   for seven   months.

A. Have you seen him   since   his wedding?

B. I've seen him   only   once.

SINCE WHEN?

1. _____I'm_____ sick today.

   ___I've been sick___ since I got up this morning.

2. Rita _____ a swollen knee.

   _____ a swollen knee since she played soccer last Saturday.

3. Roger _____ how to ski.

   _____ how to ski since he took lessons last winter.

4. _____ nervous.

   _____ nervous since they got married a few hours ago.

5. _____ lost.

   _____ lost since we arrived here this morning.

6. I _____ a stiff neck.

   _____ a stiff neck since I went to a tennis match yesterday.

7. _____ cold and cloudy.

   _____ cold and cloudy since we got here last weekend.

8. My daughter _____ the cello.

   _____ played the cello since she was six years old.

9. My boyfriend _____ bored.

   _____ bored since the concert began forty-five minutes ago.

10. _____ afraid of dogs.

   _____ afraid of dogs since my neighbor's dog bit me last year.

Listen and choose the correct answer.

1. a. Bob is in the army.
   (b.) Bob is engaged.

2. a. Carol is in music school.
   b. Carol is a professional musician.

3. a. Michael has been home for a week.
   b. Michael hurt himself this week.

4. a. She hasn't started her new job.
   b. She gets up early every morning.

5. a. Richard is in college.
   b. Richard hasn't eaten in the cafeteria.

6. a. Nancy and Tom met five and a half years ago.
   b. Nancy and Tom met when they were five and a half years old.

7. a. They play soccer every weekend.
   b. They're eight years old.

8. a. Patty is a teenager.
   b. Patty has short hair.

9. a. Ron used to own his own business.
   b. Ron moved nine years ago.

10. a. She's interested in astronomy.
    b. She's eleven years old.

11. a. He's in high school.
    b. He isn't in high school now.

12. a. Alan has owned his house for fifteen years.
    b. Alan doesn't have problems with his house now.

F CROSSWORD

| dizzy | fever | measles | nauseous | sore | stiff |

Across

3. My throat has been very _____ since Tuesday.
4. I haven't been able to eat since yesterday. I feel _____.
6. I've had a _____ neck for a week.

Down

1. I've had a high _____ for 24 hours.
2. My children have had little red spots all over their bodies for two days. They have the _____.
5. I've been _____ since I fell down and hurt my head.

G SCRAMBLED SENTENCES

Unscramble the sentences.

1. she a jazz Julie liked teenager. has was since

   Julie has liked jazz since she was a teenager.

2. he play little the since known a boy. He's piano was how to

   _____

3. since I've was in I astronomy young. interested been

   _____

4. since been they college. engaged They've finished

   _____

5. been he a cooking He's graduated from chef school. since

   _____

6. she wanted be to teacher eighteen She's a years since old. was

   _____

7. moved ago. business They've their year owned since a they here own

   _____

H WRITE ABOUT YOURSELF

1. I'm interested in ....

   I've been interested in .... since ....

2. I own ....

   I've owned .... since ....

3. I like ....

   I've .... since ....

4. I want to ....

   I've .... since ....

5. I know how to ....

   I've .... since ....

THEN AND NOW

be	have	speak	teach	visit	walk

1. Mr. and Mrs. Miller __walk__ every day.

_____ every day since Mr. Miller had problems with his heart last

year. Before that, _____ never

_____. They stayed home and watched TV.

2. Sam _____ with a Boston accent.

_____ with a Boston accent since he moved to Boston last summer.

Before that, _____ with a New York accent.

3. Terry _____ a truck driver. She drives a truck between the east coast

and the west coast. _____ a truck driver for a year. Before that,

_____ a taxi driver.

4. Before he moved to Brazil, Professor Baker

_____ French. Now _____

English. _____ English at a Brazilian university for the past two years.

5. Your Uncle Walter _____ already

_____ us five times this year!

Last year, he _____ us only twice. How many times will he

_____ us next year?!

6. Tiffany _____ long blond hair.

_____ long blond hair since she became a movie star. Before that, she

_____ short brown hair. Tiffany looks very different now!

LOOKING BACK

Victor
(be)

musician   1990–now
photographer   1982–1989

1. How long _____*has Victor been*_____ a musician?

    _____*He's been a musician*_____ since ____*1990*____.

2. How long _____*was he*_____ a photographer?

    _____*He was a photographer*_____ for ____*7 years*____.

Mrs. Sanchez
(teach)

science   1995–now
math   1985–1994

3. How long _____ science?

    _____ since _____.

4. How long _____ math?

    _____ for _____.

my grandparents
(have)

dog   1998–now
cat   1986–1997

5. How long _____ a cat?

    _____ for _____.

6. How long _____ a dog?

    _____ since _____.

Betty
(work)

bank   2000–now
mall   1997–1999

7. How long _____ at the bank?

    _____ since _____.

8. How long _____ at the mall?

    _____ for _____.

my parents
(live)

Miami   2001–now
New York 1980–2000

9. How long _____ in New York?

    _____ for _____.

10. How long _____ in Miami?

    _____ since _____.

1. Do you still go skiing every winter?

No. ....
.... (for/since) ....
....

2. Do you still live ....
.... ?

No. ....
.... (for/since) ....
....

3. Are you still a/an ....
.... ?

No. ....
.... (for/since) ....
....

4. How long have you been interested in
.... ?

....
.... (for/since) ....
....

5. Do you still ....
.... in your free time?

No. ....
.... (for/since) ....
....

6. Do your brothers still call you "Tiny Tim"?

No. ....

.... (for/since) ....

....

7. How long have you ....

....

.... ?

....

.... (for/since) ....

....

8. Do you still ....

....

.... ?

No. ....

.... (for/since) ....

....

LISTENING 🔊

Listen and choose the correct answer.

1. a. He's always been a salesperson.
    (b.) He was a cashier.

2. a. His daughter was in medical school.
    b. His daughter is in medical school.

3. a. Her parents haven't always lived in a house.
    b. Her parents have always lived in a house.

4. a. He's always wanted to be an actor.
    b. He isn't in college now.

5. a. They exercise at their health club every day.
    b. They haven't exercised at their health club since last year.

6. a. James hasn't always been a bachelor.
    b. James has been married for ten years.

7. a. Jane has wanted to meet a writer.
    b. Jane wants to be a writer.

8. a. He's never broken his ankle.
    b. He's never sprained his ankle.

9. a. She's always liked rock music.
    b. She hasn't always liked classical music.

10. a. Billy has had a fever for two days.
    b. Billy has had a sore throat for two days.

11. a. Jennifer has always been the manager.
    b. Jennifer hasn't been a salesperson since last fall.

12. a. He's interested in modern art now.
    b. He's always been interested in art.

Read the article on student book page 65 and answer the questions.

1. A "24/7" company is open _____.
   a. 365 days a year
   b. 24 days a month
   c. 7 hours a day
   d. 24 weeks a year

2. The _____ is NOT an example of instant communication.
   a. telephone   c. mail
   b. fax   d. Internet

3. About 80% of all employees work _____.
   a. from 3:00 P.M. to 11:00 P.M.
   b. from 9:00 A.M. to 5:00 P.M.
   c. from 11:00 P.M. to 7:00 A.M.
   d. from 5:00 P.M. to 9:00 A.M.

4. International companies operate 24 hours a day because _____.
   a. they take care of emergencies
   b. many people like to work at night
   c. their employees need the money
   d. they have customers in different time zones

5. Until recently _____ have had a traditional daytime schedule.
   a. factory workers
   b. office workers
   c. firefighters
   d. nurses

6. When a local laundromat stays open 24 hours a day, it's probably because _____.
   a. its customers work different shifts
   b. its customers use the Internet
   c. it's an international company
   d. it sells products worldwide

7. According to this article, an employee of a "24/7" company _____.
   a. has to travel to other countries
   b. has to work 24 hours a day
   c. might have to work at night
   d. has to work overtime

8. The main idea of this article is _____.
   a. most businesses are open all day
   b. people work harder than they used to
   c. technology is creating more jobs
   d. technology is changing employees' work schedules

9. Which of these details DOES NOT support the main idea of the article?
   a. Many companies sell products worldwide.
   b. Local businesses have adjusted their hours.
   c. Some employees have switched to other shifts.
   d. Doctors and nurses work at night.

10. The purpose of this article is _____.
    a. to recommend types of jobs
    b. to describe changes in when people work
    c. to help night shift workers
    d. to complain about technology

B FACT FILE

Look at the Fact File on student book page 67 and answer the questions.

1. In _____ of the six countries, workers typically receive less than a month of vacation time.
   a. two
   b. three
   c. four
   d. five

2. A typical employee in Australia has _____ vacation time as a typical employee in the United States.
   a. the same amount of
   b. twice as much
   c. three times as much
   d. four times as much

C INTERVIEW

Read the interview on student book page 66 and answer the questions.

1. Mr. Souza gets to work at _____.
   a. 5:30 A.M.
   b. 6:30 A.M.
   c. 7:00 A.M.
   d. 3:00 P.M.

2. At 2:30 P.M., the children are _____.
   a. with their grandmother
   b. with their mother
   c. with their father
   d. at daycare

3. Mrs. Souza DOESN'T _____.
   a. do housework
   b. eat dinner with her children
   c. take the children to her mother's
   d. eat breakfast with her children

4. When Mr. Souza leaves work, his wife is _____.
   a. getting up
   b. doing housework
   c. starting work
   d. picking up the children

5. Mr. and Mrs. Souza spend time together _____.
   a. in the morning
   b. in the afternoon
   c. in the evening
   d. on the weekend

6. Mr. and Mrs. Souza can't communicate easily with each other because _____.
   a. they have too much housework
   b. their work schedules are different
   c. they don't write messages
   d. they don't have a telephone

7. Mr. Souza is probably asleep by 10:00 P.M. because _____.
   a. he doesn't have anything to do
   b. he lives on a quiet street
   c. he has to get up very early
   d. he doesn't want to wake up his wife

8. You can conclude that _____.
   a. the Souzas' children stay up late
   b. Mr. Souza likes his job
   c. Mrs. Souza is looking for a new job
   d. Mr. and Mrs. Souza work hard

D YOU'RE THE INTERVIEWER!

Interview a classmate, a neighbor, or a friend. Use the chart below to record the person's answers. Then share what you learned with the class.

Describe your typical day.	
When do you spend time with your family?	
What do you like about your schedule?	
What *don't* you like about your schedule?	

FUN WITH IDIOMS: What's the Expression?

Choose the correct idiom to describe each person.

a couch potato	a real peach	chicken
a real ham	a smart cookie	the top banana

1. Roy is afraid to ask for a better work schedule. He's _____.

2. Lucy sits around and watches television all day. She's _____.

3. Edward is the funniest person I know. He's _____.

4. Miranda is the head of our company. She's _____.

5. Everyone loves Sally. She's _____.

6. Nancy knows more about computers than her teacher. She's _____.

F **FUN WITH IDIOMS: Crossword**

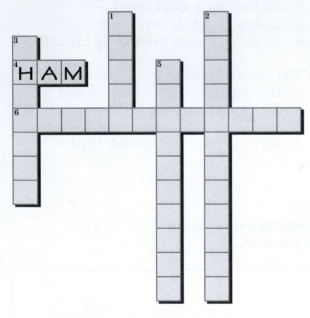

Across

4. A funny person is a _____.

6. A lazy person is a _____.

Down

1. A nice person is a _____.
2. An intelligent person is a _____.
3. A person who is afraid is _____.
5. The boss is the _____.

G **FUN WITH IDIOMS: Writing**

Do you know someone who is a ham? a real peach? a smart cookie? the top banana? Write about a person who "fits" one of these descriptions. Explain the reasons for your answer. Then share with your classmates.

H **WE'VE GOT MAIL!**

Choose the words that best complete each sentence.

1. I've already _____ dinner.
   a. eat   c. eaten
   b. eating   d. ate

2. He's never _____ a first-aid course.
   a. took   c. takes
   b. taking   d. taken

(continued)

3. Randy hasn't _____ his homework yet.
   a. doing   c. did
   b. done   d. to do

4. She's _____ a teacher for a long time.
   a. was   c. already
   b. being   d. been

5. I've _____ to Chicago many times.
   a. driving   c. driven
   b. drove   d. went

6. _____ at this company since last year.
   a. I've worked   c. I worked
   b. I'm working   d. I work

Choose the sentence that is correct and complete.

7. a. I wasn't gone to the store yet.
   b. I haven't gone to the store yet.
   c. I haven't went to the store yet.
   d. I didn't gone to the store yet.

8. a. I've known Mary since I was young.
   b. I knew Mary since I've been young.
   c. I'm knowing Mary since I was young.
   d. I know Mary since I've been young.

9. a. I'm interested in art for many years.
   b. I'm being interested in art for many years.
   c. I've being interested in art for many years.
   d. I've been interested in art for many years.

10. a. We've already saw that play.
    b. We already seen that play.
    c. We've already seen that play.
    d. We're already seen that play.

11. a. They've never flown in an airplane.
    b. They've never flew in an airplane.
    c. They haven't never flown in an airplane.
    d. They never flown in an airplane.

12. a. She's speaking English for a year.
    b. She has spoken English for a year.
    c. She have spoken English for a year.
    d. She is spoken English for a year.

"CAN-DO" REVIEW

Match the "can do" statement and the correct sentence.

_____ 1. I can ask about a person's skills.

_____ 2. I can describe my work experience.

_____ 3. I can describe actions that have already occurred.

_____ 4. I can describe actions that haven't occurred yet.

_____ 5. I can ask about likes.

_____ 6. I can ask about a person's health.

_____ 7. I can describe an ailment or symptom.

_____ 8. I can tell about the duration of an illness.

_____ 9. I can react to information.

_____ 10. I can ask about the duration of an activity.

a. I haven't fed the dog yet.

b. I have a pain in my back.

c. How are you feeling?

d. I've written business reports for many years.

e. How long have you been interested in photography?

f. Do you like to swim?

g. Oh. I wasn't aware of that.

h. Do you know how to do yoga?

i. I've been sick for a week.

j. I've already gone to the supermarket today.

for	since

1. We've been living here ___since___ 2001.

2. It's been raining _____ two days.

3. I've been listening to this music _____ an hour.

4. She's been flying airplanes _____ 1995.

5. Billy, you've been roller-blading _____ this morning!

6. He's been practicing the cello _____ three and a half hours.

7. Our neighbors have been vacuuming

   _____ 7 A.M.

8. We've been having problems with our

   heat _____ a week.

B CHOOSE

1. I've been working here since _____.
   - (a) last month
   - b. three months

2. He's been taking a shower for _____.
   - a. this afternoon
   - b. half an hour

3. It's been ringing for _____.
   - a. two o'clock
   - b. a few minutes

4. She's been studying since _____.
   - a. eight o'clock
   - b. an hour

5. They've been dating for _____.
   - a. high school
   - b. six months

6. I've been feeling sick since _____.
   - a. twelve hours
   - b. yesterday

1. How long have you been studying?

   _____I've been studying since_____
   early this morning.

3. How long has Tom been having problems
   with his car?

   _____
   a week.

5. How long have we been waiting?

   _____
   forty-five minutes.

7. How long has Professor Drake been
   talking?

   _____
   an hour and a half.

9. How long have you been teaching?

   _____
   1975.

2. How long has Ann been feeling sick?

   _____
   a few days.

4. How long have the people next door been
   arguing?

   _____
   last night.

6. How long has that cell phone been ringing?

   _____
   the play began.

8. How long have Rick and Sally been
   dating?

   _____
   high school.

10. How long have I been chatting online?

    _____
    more than two hours.

D WHAT ARE THEY DOING?

assemble	bake	bark	browse	do	jog	look	make	plant

1. Larry _____is looking_____ for his keys.

   _____He's been looking_____ for his keys all morning.

2. My sister _____ in the park.

   _____ in the park since 8 A.M.

3. The dog next door _____.

   _____ all day.

4. Our neighbors _____ flowers.

   _____ flowers for several hours.

5. Michael _____ his homework.

   _____ his homework since dinner.

6. My wife _____ the web.

   _____ the web for an hour.

7. Mr. and Mrs. Lee _____ their son's new bicycle.

   _____ it all afternoon.

8. I'm _____ cookies.

   _____ cookies since two o'clock.

9. You and your brother _____ a lot of noise!

   _____ noise since you got up.

E LISTENING

Listen and choose the correct time expressions to complete the sentences.

1. a. 1995.
   b. a few years.

2. a. 1:45.
   b. forty-five minutes.

3. a. 3 o'clock.
   b. thirty minutes.

4. a. yesterday.
   b. several days.

5. a. 7:30 this morning.
   b. more than an hour.

6. a. 7 o'clock.
   b. a half hour.

7. a. a few weeks.
   b. last month.

8. a. about three hours.
   b. 4 o'clock.

9. a. early this morning.
   b. twenty minutes.

F **GRAMMARRAP:** *How Long?*

Listen. Then clap and practice.

A.   How long have you been   working   at the mall?

B.   I've been working   at the mall   since the fall.

A.   How long has she been   wearing   her new ring?

B.   She's been wearing   her new ring   since the spring.

A.   How long have you been   living   in L.A.?

B.   We've been living   in L.A.   since May.

A.   How long has he been   waiting   for the train?

B.   He's been waiting   since it started   to rain.

A.   How long have you been   looking for   that mouse?

B.   We've been looking   since we rented   this house.

Activity Workbook   **65**

G WHAT ARE THEY SAYING?

| make | play | run | snow | study | take | vacuum | wait | wear | work |

1. Excuse me. **Have you been waiting** in line for a long time?

   Yes, I **have**. **I've been waiting** for more than an hour.

2. What a terrible day! _____ for a long time?

   Yes, _____. since early this morning.

3. Your son plays the violin very beautifully. _____ lessons for a long time?

   Yes, _____. lessons since he was five.

4. _____ here for a long time?

   No, _____. I've _____ here for only a week.

5. _____ your car _____ strange noises for a long time?

   Yes, _____. these noises all week.

6. You look tired. _____ for a long time?

   Yes, _____. all morning.

7. Your children speak French very well. _____ it for a long time?

Yes, _____. _____ French for six years.

8. I'm really tired. _____ for a long time?

Yes, we _____. _____ since 6 A.M.

9. Your pants are dirty. _____ them all week?

No, _____. _____ them for only a few hours.

10. This is the sixth game you've won today. _____ for a long time?

No, _____. _____ for only a few months.

Listen and choose what the people are talking about.

1. a. traffic
   b. a computer

2. a. a wall
   b. the furniture

3. a. the guitar
   b. my bills

4. a. the drums
   b. tennis

5. a. the cookies
   b. the babies

6. a. the cake
   b. the bridge

7. a. her composition
   b. her bicycle

8. a. books
   b. trains

9. a. a sandwich
   b. a novel

10. a. socks
    b. chairs

11. a. the president
    b. songs

12. a. a restaurant
    b. a neighbor

13. a. fruit
    b. my car

14. a. a test
    b. a cake

15. a. videos
    b. problems

Listen to each word and then say it.

this			these		
1. bills	3. chicken	5. building	1. week	3. briefcase	5. fever
2. officer	4. ticket	6. itself	2. speak	4. friendly	6. eaten

Listen and put a circle around the word that has the same sound.

1. thin:	police	tired	(interested)
2. build:	headache	is	sweater
3. read:	Steve's	been	try
4. if:	in	bite	taxi
5. live:	met	history	child
6. fishing:	science	writing	sister
7. piece:	very	wear	winter
8. east:	hire	Chinese	ready

Now make a sentence using all the words you circled, and read the sentence aloud.

9. ....

10. key:	dinner	receive	think
11. tennis:	easy	heater	this
12. complete:	any	get	try
13. keep:	busy	Peter	disturb
14. tuxedo:	type	if	week
15. Linda:	didn't	green	bright
16. meeting:	child	forget	e-mail

Now make a sentence using all the words you circled, and read the sentence aloud.

17. ....

J YOU DECIDE: *What Have They Been Doing?*

1. I have a sore throat.

   No wonder you have a sore throat!

   .... You've been singing .... all day.

2. My back hurts.

   No wonder your back hurts!

   .... all day.

3. Bob has a terrible sunburn.

   No wonder he has a terrible sunburn!

   .... all day.

4. Nancy is very tired.

   No wonder she's very tired!

   .... all day.

5. Jane and I have headaches.

   No wonder you have headaches!

   .... all day.

6. Bob and Judy are very disappointed.

   No wonder they're very disappointed!

   .... all day.

7. I can't finish my dinner.

   No wonder you can't finish your dinner!

   .... all day.

8. Victor doesn't have any money.

   No wonder he doesn't have any money!

   .... all day.

complain	eat	go	make	read	see	study	swim	talk	write

1. My husband and I are very full. ___We've been eating___ for the
past two hours. ___We've___ already ___eaten___ soup, salad,
chicken, and vegetables. And our dinner isn't finished.
___We haven't eaten___ our dessert yet!

2. Dr. Davis is tired. _____ patients since early
this morning. _____ already _____ twenty patients,
and it's only two o'clock. _____ the other
patients in her waiting room yet.

3. Dave likes to swim. _____ for an hour
and a half. _____ already _____ across the pool thirty
times.

4. Amy is very tired. _____ to job interviews for
the past three weeks. _____ already _____ to ten job
interviews, and she hasn't found a job yet!

5. Gregory loves to talk. _____ all evening.
_____ already _____ about his job, his house, and his
car. Fortunately, _____ about his cats yet.

6. Betty and Bob are writing thank-you notes for their wedding gifts,
and they're very tired. _____ them all weekend.
_____ already _____ to their aunts, uncles, and
cousins, but _____ to their friends yet.

7. Andrew is tired. He's having a party tonight, and _____ _____ desserts since early this morning. _____ already _____ two apple pies and three blueberry pies. But he isn't finished. _____ a chocolate cake yet.

8. Patty is very tired. _____ since she got home from school. _____ already _____ English and math. And she'll be up late tonight because _____ for her history test yet.

9. Today is Howard's day off, and he's enjoying himself. _____ _____ since early this morning. _____ already _____ three short stories. But _____ today's newspaper yet.

10. Mr. and Mrs. Grumble like to complain. _____ all evening. _____ already _____ about their jobs, the weather, and several members of their family. Fortunately, they _____ about the party yet, but I'm sure they will.

L LISTENING 🔊

Listen and decide where the conversation is taking place.

1. (a.) in a kitchen
   b. in a supermarket

2. a. at home
   b. in school

3. a. in a department store
   b. in a laundromat

4. a. at a movie theater
   b. at home

5. a. at a clinic
   b. at a bakery

6. a. in a cafeteria
   b. in a library

7. a. at a concert hall
   b. at a museum

8. a. at a health club
   b. in a book store

9. a. in an office
   b. at a bus stop

10. a. at a zoo
    b. in a pet shop

11. a. at home
    b. at a movie theater

12. a. at a clinic
    b. in a department store

WHICH WORD?

1. The floor is wet! How long has the ceiling been (leaking) / leaked ?

2. I'm not nervous. I've been flown / flying in helicopters for years.

3. I'm a little worried. I've never been running / run in a marathon before.

4. How many pizzas have you already made / been making so far today?

5. You look tired. What have you / have you been doing today?

6. I think I've seen / been seeing this movie before.

7. Has your husband already giving / given blood?

8. I've never taken / been taking a karate lesson. Have you?

9. Have you ever been going / gone out on a date before?

10. Alexander, your cell phone has rung / has been ringing since we started class!

11. Jane isn't nervous. She's been sung / singing in front of audiences for years.

YOU DECIDE: *What Are They Saying?*

A. Mrs. Vickers, could I speak to you for a few minutes?

B. Of course. Please sit down.

A. Mrs. Vickers, I've been thinking. I've been working here at the

.... Company (for/since) ....
I've worked very hard, and I've done a lot of things here.

For example, I've ....,

I've ....,

and I've been ....

(for/since) ....

B. That's true, Mr. Mills. And we're happy with your work.

A. Thank you, Mrs. Vickers. As I was saying, I know I've done a very good job here, and I really think I should get a raise.

I haven't had a raise (for/since) ....

B. ....

A. ....

A. Dad, could I speak to you for a few minutes?

B. Sure, James. Please sit down.

A. Dad, I've been thinking. I've been working very hard in school this year, and I've done all my chores at home. For example,

I've ...., I've ....

.................................., and I've been ....

.... (for/since) ....

B. That's true, James. Your mother and I are very proud of you.

A. Thank you, Dad. As I was saying, I know I've been very responsible, and I really think I should be able to take your car when I go out on a date. After all, I've been driving

(for/since) ....

B. ....

A. ....

A NEW LIFE

Daniel has been living in a small town in Mexico all his life. His father just got a good job in the United States, and Daniel and his family are going to live there. Daniel's life is going to be very different in the United States.

1. He's going to live in a big city.
2. He's going to take English lessons.
3. He's going to take the subway.
4. He's going to shop in American supermarkets.
5. He's going to eat American food.
6. He's going to play American football.

7. He's going to ....

Daniel is a little nervous.

1. _____*He's never lived in a big city*_____ before.

2. _____ before.

3. _____ before.

4. _____ before.

5. _____ before.

6. _____ before.

7. .... before.

Daniel's cousins have been living in the United States for many years. They'll be able to help him.

8. _____*They've been living in a big city*_____ for years.

9. _____ for years.

10. _____ for years.

11. _____ for years.

12. _____ for years.

13. _____ for years.

14. .... for years.

Daniel's cousins tell him he shouldn't worry. They're sure he'll enjoy his new life in the United States very much.

YOU DECIDE: *A New Life*

.... has been living in ....
all her life. Now she's going to move to ....
(your city)

Her life is going to be very different in ....
(your city)

1. She's going to ....
2. She's going to ....
3. She's going to ....
4. She's going to ....
5. She's going to ....

_____ is a little nervous.

6. _____ before.
7. _____ before.
8. _____ before.
9. _____ before.
10. _____ before.

.... (has/have) been living in _____ for many
years and will be able to help her.

11. _____ for years.
12. _____ for years.
13. _____ for years.
14. _____ for years.
15. _____ for years.

_____ shouldn't worry. I'm sure she'll enjoy her new life in _____
very much.

✔ CHECK-UP TEST: Chapters 4–6

A. Complete the sentences with the present perfect.

Ex. *(do)* Julie ___has___ already ___done___ her homework.

(read) I ___haven't read___ your report yet.

(eat) **1.** Mary and her brother _____ already _____ breakfast.

(take) **2.** My nephew _____ his violin lesson yet.

(write) **3.** I _____ to my grandparents yet.

(go) **4.** My wife _____ already _____ to work.

(pay) **5.** You _____ your electric bill yet.

(have) **6.** Henry _____ already _____ a problem with his new cell phone.

B. Complete the questions.

1. A. _____ to your supervisor yet?

   B. Yes, I have. I spoke to her this morning.

2. A. _____ his new bicycle yet?

   B. Yes, he has. He rode it this morning.

3. A. _____ their paychecks yet?

   B. Yes, they have. They got them this afternoon.

4. A. _____ ever _____ in a helicopter?

   B. Yes, he has. He flew in a helicopter last summer.

5. A. _____ ever _____ on TV?

   B. Yes, she has. She was on TV last week.

6. A. _____ your daughter's new boyfriend yet?

   B. No, I haven't. I'm going to meet him tonight.

C. Complete the sentences.

Ex. My neck is very stiff. _____It's been_____ stiff since I got up this morning.

   Tom is reading his e-mail. ___He's been reading___ it for a half hour.

1. It's sunny. _____ all week.

2. We're browsing the web. _____ the web since 8 o'clock.

3. My daughter has a fever. _____ a fever since early this morning.

4. My son is studying. _____ since he got home from school.

5. Our neighbors are arguing. _____ all afternoon.

6. I know how to skate. _____ how to skate since I was six years old.

7. Susan is interested in science. _____ interested in science since she was a teenager.

8. My husband and I are cleaning our basement. _____ it all weekend.

D. **Complete the answers.**

| for | since |

1. How long has your wife been working at the bank?

_____ 1999.

2. How long have those dogs been barking?

_____ a long time.

3. How long has it been snowing?

_____ two days.

4. How long have you wanted to be an astronaut?

_____ I was six years old.

E. **Complete the sentences.**

1. My brother owns a motorcycle. _____ a motorcycle since last summer.

Before that, _____ a bicycle.

2. I'm a journalist. _____ a journalist since 2000.

Before that, _____ an actor.

3. My daughter likes classical music. _____ classical music since she finished college.

Before that, _____ rock music.

F. **Listen and choose the correct answer.** 🔊

1. a. Janet is in acting school.
  b. Janet is an actress.

2. a. The president has finished his speech.
  b. The president is still speaking.

3. a. They've been living in New York since 1995.
  b. They haven't lived in New York since 1995.

4. a. They're going to eat later.
  b. They're going to eat now.

5. a. She's called the superintendent.
  b. She has to call the superintendent.

6. a. Someone is helping Billy with his homework.
  b. No one is helping Billy with his homework.

A WHAT DO THEY { ENJOY DOING / LIKE TO DO } ?

| enjoy _____ing | like to _____ | _____ing |

1. My wife and I _____enjoy_____ relaxing on the beach when we go on vacation.

2. Mrs. Finn is very talkative. She _____likes to_____ talk about her grandchildren.

   _____Talking_____ about her grandchildren is important to her.

3. Billy doesn't _____ going to the doctor, but he went yesterday for his annual checkup.

4. I _____ knit sweaters. _____ sweaters is a good way to relax.

5. My husband doesn't _____ asking for a raise, but sometimes he has to.

6. Dr. Brown _____ deliver babies. In her opinion, _____ babies is the best job in the world.

7. Bob doesn't _____ being a bachelor. He thinks _____ married is better.

8. Ann _____ plant flowers. She thinks _____ flowers is good exercise.

9. Jim _____ chatting online with his friends, but his parents think _____ online every evening isn't a very good idea.

10. Tom doesn't _____ play hockey. He thinks _____ hockey is dangerous.

11. My parents go to the gym during the winter, but in the summer they _____ going hiking.

12. Martin _____ go to parties. He thinks _____ to parties is a good way to meet people.

13. I really want to play the piano well, but I don't _____ practicing.

Listen. Then clap and practice.

Writing is   fun.

I like to   write.

I enjoy   writing letters   late   at night.

Eating is   fun.

I like to   eat.

I enjoy eating   fish,   and I like eating   meat.

Skiing is   great.

He likes to   ski.

But skiing's been   hard   since he hurt   his knee.

Singing is   fun.

She likes to   sing.

But today   she's sick,   and she can't sing   a thing.

Running is   great.

They like to   run.

Swimming's   okay,   but running's   more fun.

Baking is   great.

He likes to   bake.

When he's feeling   sad,   he bakes   a cake.

Knitting is   fun.

She likes to   knit.

She enjoys knitting   sweaters,   but none of them   fit!

C WHAT'S THE WORD?

clean	complain	eat	go	sit	wear
cleaning	complaining	eating	going	sitting	wearing

1. I hate to _____complain_____, but your loud music is disturbing me.

2. Carol tries to avoid _____ in the sun.

3. Sally likes to _____ dinner at home.

4. My son hates to _____ his room.

5. Richard can't stand to _____ a tie.

6. Tom avoids _____ his apartment whenever he can.

7. James doesn't like to _____ to the mall.

8. My husband and I hate _____ sailing.

9. My wife and I like to _____ in the park on a sunny day.

10. Please try to avoid _____ about the weather all the time.

11. My friends and I can't stand _____ in fast-food restaurants.

12. My daughter likes _____ the sweater you gave her for her birthday.

D GRAMMARRAP: *Pet Peeves*

Listen. Then clap and practice.

I don't like	waiting	for the bus	in the rain.
I hate to	rush	when I'm late	for a plane.
I avoid	talking	to strangers	on the train.
I can't stand	driving	in the center	lane.

I don't like to	iron	on a hot	summer day.
I hate to clean	the house	in the middle	of May.
I avoid	dusting	and sweeping	my floors.
I can't stand	doing	all my household	chores!

YOU DECIDE: *What's the Reason?*

1. David is happy he works in a gym because he enjoys

   exercising every day.

2. Gloria hates being a taxi driver because she can't stand

   .

3. Miguel is glad he lives in Puerto Rico because he likes

   .

4. I'm sorry I'm a secretary because I can't stand

   .

5. We're happy we're going camping because we enjoy

   .

6. William is upset he's sick because he hates

   .

7. I'm glad I have a new bicycle because I like

   .

8. Norman doesn't like being on a diet because he can't stand

   .

9. Julie is happy she's a Hollywood actress because she enjoys

   .

F MY ENERGETIC GRANDFATHER

A. Your grandfather is very energetic!

B. He sure is!

A. When did he start _____ ¹ the drums?

B. Believe it or not, he learned _____ ² the drums when he was sixty years old!

A. That's incredible! Does he _____ ³ the drums often?

B. Yes, he does. He's played every day for the last eight years.

A. What else does he enjoy doing?

B. He enjoys _____ ⁴, he enjoys _____ ⁵,

and he also enjoys _____ ⁶.

A. I hope I have that much energy when I'm his age!

G I CAN'T STAND IT!

I spoke with my friend Pam last weekend, and she talked a lot about figure skating. Ever since she started to figure skate several months ago, that's all she ever talks about! I never go out with her anymore because she practices figure skating all the time. And whenever I talk to her on the phone, figure skating is the only thing she talks about! (She thinks that everybody should learn to figure skate.) I can't stand it! I don't ever want to hear another word about figure skating!

Now YOU tell about somebody.

I spoke to my friend .... last weekend, and .... talked a lot about

.... Ever since ....

....

....

....

....

....

1. I've decided [buy / buying / (to buy)] a motorcycle.

4. You should consider [to change / change / changing] jobs.

2. Have you ever considered [to move / moving / move] ?

5. Have you decided to [get / to get / getting] a dog?

3. I'm thinking about [going / to go / go] on a diet.

6. He's thought about [to retire / retiring / retire] .

I **GRAMMARRAP**: *I Considered Ordering the Cheesecake*

Listen. Then clap and practice.

I considered   ordering the cheesecake.
Everyone   said I should   try it.
But then   I decided   to skip   dessert.
I wanted to   stay   on my diet.

I thought about   going   home early.
It was only   a quarter to   ten.
But I changed   my mind and   decided to   stay
When the music   started   again.

I thought about   moving to   France
And studying   music and   dance.
But I changed   my mind and   decided to   stay
With my cat   and my bird and my   plants.

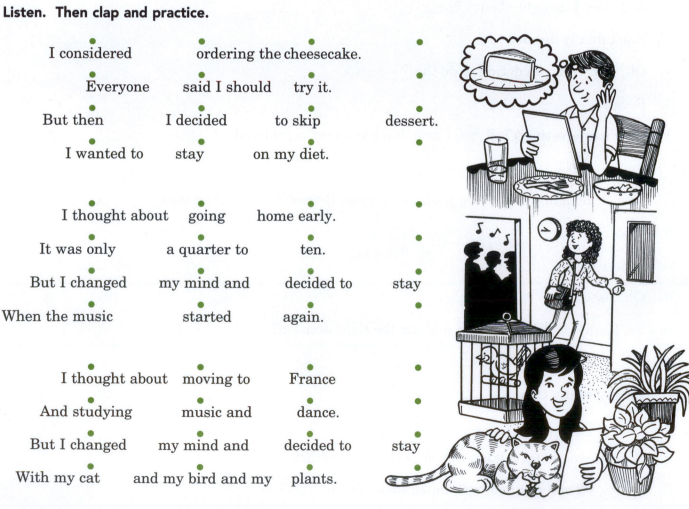

J **YOU DECIDE:** *What's Carla Going to Do?*

A. Hi, Carla. How are you? We haven't spoken in a long time. Tell me, what have you been doing?

B. ....

A. Oh. And what are you thinking about doing after you finish studying English?

B. For a while, I considered .... ,

and then I thought about ....

But I finally decided to ....

A. Oh. Why did you decide to do that?

B. Because ....

A. That's interesting. Tell me, Carla, have you ever considered ....

.... ?

B. Yes. I thought about doing that, but decided it wasn't a very good idea.

A. Why not?

B. Because ....

A. Oh, I see.

B. So, Kathy, do you think I'm making the right decision?

A. ....

B. Do you really think so?

A. ....

B. Well, it was great talking to you. Let's get together soon.

A. Okay. I'll call you and we'll make some plans.

84 **Activity Workbook**

1. You can't keep on _____rearranging_____ the furniture so often. You rearranged it last weekend!

2. I stopped _____ meat. I only eat fish and chicken.

3. He tried to quit _____, but he couldn't. He still worries about everything.

4. Alice always gets up late. She should start _____ up earlier.

5. Richard doesn't exercise very often. He should begin _____ every day. He'll feel a lot better.

6. You can't continue _____ me the same question. You've already asked me ten times!

7. I realize that I can't keep on _____ with people. I'm never going to argue with anyone again!

8. I know that Dave takes piano lessons. When did he start _____ guitar lessons?

9. You should stop _____ your bills late and start _____ them on time.

10. Professor Blaine is very boring. Students continue _____ asleep in his classes.

L **GOOD DECISIONS**

| bite | clean | cook | do | gossip | interrupt | make | pay |

This year I'm going to break all my bad habits. First, I've decided to stop _____biting_____ [1] my nails. I've also started _____ [2] exercises every day. I learned _____ [3] when I was young, so I've decided to start _____ [4] healthy meals. I'm also considering _____ [5] my bills on time, and I'm thinking about _____ [6] my apartment every week. I've also decided to stop _____ [7] about other people and to stop _____ [8] my friends while they're talking.

1.
My husband can't stop _____falling_____ asleep at the movies. Every

time we go, he falls asleep. If he keeps on _____ asleep,
I'll never go to a movie with him again.

2.
I don't think I should continue _____ weights every day. I

like _____ weights, but I'm afraid I might hurt my back if I

keep on _____ them so often.

3.
My older sister always teases me. Today I'm really mad! She began

_____ me early this morning, and she hasn't stopped. If

she keeps on _____ me, I'm going to cry. And I won't

stop _____ until she stops _____ me!

4.
My friend Albert has got to stop _____ so fast and start

_____ more carefully. If he continues _____
fast, I'm sure he'll have a serious accident some day.

5.
Mr. Perkins, when are you going to stop _____ so sloppily

and start _____ more neatly? If you keep on

_____ like that, I'm going to have to fire you.

6.
My boyfriend is very clumsy. When we go dancing, he keeps on

_____ on my feet. If he doesn't start _____

more gracefully, I'm going to stop _____ dancing with him.

Listen and choose the correct answer.

1. a. delivering babies.
    b. fix broken legs.

2. a. eating junk food.
    b. to pay our bills late.

3. a. swimming.
    b. to play golf.

4. a. to tap dance.
    b. figure skating.

5. a. to work out at a health club every week.
    b. retiring.

6. a. taking karate lessons.
    b. mend my pants.

7. a. to go back to college?
    b. moving?

8. a. to argue with people.
    b. biting my nails.

9. a. teasing your sister?
    b. to go to bed so late?

10. a. eat fruits and vegetables.
    b. worrying about my health all the time.

11. a. stand in line.
    b. wearing a suit.

12. a. taking photographs?
    b. study the piano?

13. a. to do his homework.
    b. clean his apartment.

14. a. studying engineering.
    b. teach a computer course.

15. a. to live at home.
    b. going to school for the rest of your life.

O **WHAT DOES IT MEAN?**

Choose the correct answer.

1. My wife is very dizzy.
    a. I'm glad to hear that.
    b. How long has she been feeling sick?
    c. I guess she has a lot of things to do.

2. Peter and Nancy are vegetarians.
    a. They've quit eating vegetables.
    b. They've stopped planting flowers.
    c. They've stopped eating meat.

3. Andrew avoids talking about politics.
    a. He doesn't like talking about politics.
    b. He enjoys talking about politics.
    c. He's learning to talk about politics.

4. Shirley has worked her way to the top.
    a. She's the tallest person in her family.
    b. She's the president of her company.
    c. She works on the top floor of her building.

5. The people across the street were furious.
    a. They were embarrassed.
    b. They were awkward.
    c. They were very angry.

6. What's your present occupation?
    a. What do you do now?
    b. What are you going to do?
    c. What did you do when you were young?

7. This is my father-in-law, Mr. Kramer.
    a. He just graduated from high school.
    b. He just retired.
    c. He's seventeen years old.

8. My mother is going to mend my socks.
    a. She's going to fix them.
    b. She's going to wash them.
    c. She's going to send them to my sister.

9. You should stop gossiping.
    a. You should stop interrupting people.
    b. You should stop bumping into people.
    c. You should stop talking about people.

10. I've decided to ask for a raise.
    a. You should speak to your landlord.
    b. You should speak to your boss.
    c. You should speak to your instructor.

11. Dr. Wu has a lot of patients.
    a. That's true. She never gets angry.
    b. I know. She's a very popular doctor.
    c. That's true. She never gets sick.

12. My Uncle Gino has an Italian accent.
    a. He bought it when he went to Italy.
    b. He wears it all the time.
    c. Everybody knows he's from Italy.

1. Lisa didn't feel very well when she got up this morning because

   she *(eat)* ___had___ ___eaten___ a lot of candy before she went to bed.

2. My husband invited his boss for dinner last Friday night, and he forgot to tell me.

   Unfortunately, I *(get)* _____ already _____ tickets for a concert.

3. Our friends didn't stop showing us pictures of their grandson all evening. They

   (visit) _____ just _____ him the day before.

4. I wanted to drive to the mountains with my friends yesterday, but they *(drive)* _____

   _____ to the mountains the afternoon before.

5. Andrew wasn't very happy when I visited him yesterday. He *(cut)* _____ just _____
   himself while he was cooking dinner.

6. Alice couldn't buy the new printer she wanted because she *(spend)* _____ _____
   all her money on her vacation.

7. When my son got home from his date last night, my wife and I *(go)* _____ already

   _____ to sleep.

8. My children didn't want to eat pancakes for breakfast yesterday morning because

   I *(make)* _____ _____ pancakes the morning before.

9. I didn't see a movie with my friends last weekend because I *(see)* _____ _____
   three movies the weekend before.

10. When I got up this morning, my wife *(leave)* _____ already _____ for work.

11. Norman was upset when I saw him yesterday morning. He *(have)* _____ _____
    a big argument with his next-door neighbor the night before.

12. When I saw Jill today, she was very happy. Her boyfriend *(give)* _____ just _____
    her a beautiful bracelet for her birthday.

13. Tom couldn't lend me his dictionary the other day because he *(lose)* _____ _____
    it the week before.

Listen. Then clap and practice.

She felt very   happy   when she left   the store.
She had never   bought   a computer   before.

He looked   very nervous when he   knocked   on the door.
He had never   gone out   on a date   before.

She felt very   weak,   and her throat was   sore.
She had never   had   the flu   before.

He felt   very proud   when his guests asked for   more.
He had never   baked   a pie   before.

She felt   very foolish   when her food   hit the floor.
She had never   eaten   with chopsticks   before.

He looked   very scared   when it started to   roar.
He had never   been close   to a lion   before.

She was very   annoyed   when he started to   snore.
He had never   made   so much noise   before.

He was very   surprised   when he opened   the drawer.
He had never   seen   so much money   before.

C LATE FOR EVERYTHING

Gary Gray was very upset yesterday. He didn't get up until 9:00, and as a result, he was late for everything all day!

Last train to Centerville leaves at 9:30.

1. He got to the train station at 9:45. The train ___had___ already ___left___.

Today's meeting begins at 10:00.

2. He drove to the office and arrived late for an important meeting.

It _____ already _____.

To: garyg@go.com
From: janet@hopmail.com

Let's have lunch at 12:00. I have to go back to work at 12:45.

3. He got to the restaurant at 1:00 to meet his friend Janet for lunch. However, she _____ already _____ back to work.

Bank Closes at 3:00.

4. He got to the bank at 3:15, but he was too late. It _____ already _____.

Professor Tweedle's Lecture on Bird-Watching Starts at 4:00.

5. He got to the bird-watching lecture at 4:15. It _____ already _____.

To: garyg@go.com
From: tom@hopmail.com

I'll be leaving at 4:30. Hope to see you before then.

6. He had made plans to get together with his friend Tom. But he didn't get to Tom's office until 5:00. His friend Tom

_____ already _____.

Dear Gary,
    Our plane will be arriving at the airport at 8:10. We're looking forward to seeing you.
        Love,
        Grandma & Grandpa

7. He drove to the airport to pick up his grandmother and grandfather. He got to the airport at 8:30. Their plane

_____ already _____.

1. We got lost on the way to the party last night. We *(listen)* ____hadn't____ ____listened____ very carefully to the directions.

2. I enjoyed seeing my old friends at my high school reunion last weekend.

   I *(see)* _____ _____ them since we finished high school.

3. My wife and I decided to have a picnic in the park last Sunday. We *(have)* _____

   _____ a picnic in the park in a long time.

4. I went dancing with my girlfriend last Saturday night, and I hurt my back.

   I *(go)* _____ _____ dancing in a long time.

5. Cynthia was embarrassed at her party last night. She had invited her cousin Charles, but

   she *(remember)* _____ _____ to invite his girlfriend, Louise.

6. Frank looked terrible when I saw him yesterday. His pants were dirty, he

   (iron) _____ _____ his shirt, and he *(shave)* _____ _____ in several days.

7. Michael was very discouraged when I saw him last week. He had been on a diet for a month,

   and he *(lose)* _____ _____ any weight.

8. Sylvia fell several times while she was skiing last weekend. She *(ski)* _____

   _____ in a long time.

9. Arnold's boss fired him last week. Arnold *(get)* _____ _____ to work on time in six months.

10. Betty was very lucky she didn't miss her plane this morning. She got to the airport late, but

    the plane *(take off)* _____ _____ yet.

11. Alan did poorly on his English exam last week. I'm not surprised. He *(study)* _____

    _____ for the test.

12. Stuart enjoyed riding his bicycle last weekend. He *(ride)* _____ _____ it in a long time.

Jennifer was very busy after school yesterday.

1:00	write an English composition
2:00	study for my science test
3:00	practice the trombone
4:00	read the next history chapter
5:00	memorize my lines for the school play

What was she doing at 2:00?

1. _____ She was studying for her science test. _____

What had she already done?

2. _____ She had already written an English composition. _____

What hadn't she done yet?

3. _____ She hadn't practiced the trombone yet. _____

4. _____

5. _____

Brian had a very busy day at the office yesterday.

9:00	send an e-mail to the boss
10:00	give the employees their paychecks
11:00	hook up the new printer
1:00	write to the Bentley Company
2:00	take two packages to the post office

What was he doing at 11:00?

6. _____

What had he already done?

7. _____

8. _____

What hadn't he done yet?

9. _____

10. _____

Mr. and Mrs. Mendoza had a very busy day at home yesterday.

8:00	assemble Billy's new bicycle
9:00	fix the fence
11:00	clean the garage
2:00	repair the roof
4:00	start to build a tree house

What were they doing at 11:00?

11. _____

What had they already done?

12. _____

13. _____

What hadn't they done yet?

14. _____

15. _____

Brenda wants to lose some weight, so she had a very busy day at her health club.

9:00	do yoga
10:00	go jogging
12:00	play squash
3:00	lift weights
4:00	swim across the pool 10 times

What was she doing at 12:00?

16. _____

What had she already done?

17. _____

18. _____

What hadn't she done yet?

19. _____

20. _____

F WHAT HAD THEY BEEN DOING?

1. Professor Smith finally ended his lecture at 6:00. He *(talk)* _____ **had been talking** _____ for three hours.

2. The Millers moved out of their apartment building last week. They *(live)* _____ _____ there for several years.

3. Our daughter lost her job last week. She *(work)* _____ at the same company since she graduated from college.

4. Peter was happy when he and his girlfriend finally got married. They *(go out)* _____ _____ for eight years.

5. We were sad when Rudy's Restaurant closed. We *(plan)* _____ to eat there on our anniversary.

6. We felt very nostalgic when we went back to our hometown. We *(think about)* _____ _____ going back there for a long time.

7. My husband and I were happy when our son decided to study harder. He *(get)* _____ _____ poor grades in school.

8. Mr. Best was happy when his neighbor bought his own ladder. He *(borrow)* _____ _____ Mr. Best's ladder for many years.

9. I'm not surprised that Lenny's doctor put him on a diet. Lenny *(eat)* _____ too many fatty foods.

10. It's too bad your daughter wasn't able to perform in her violin recital last weekend. She *(rehearse)* _____ for it for a long time.

11. I'm sorry you had to cancel your trip to Hawaii. You and your wife *(look forward)* _____ _____ to it for a long time.

12. I'm so happy that Sally won the marathon last weekend. She *(train)* _____ for it for the past six months.

13. Nobody at the office was surprised when Mrs. Anderson fired Frank, her new assistant. He *(arrive)* _____ late for work every day for the past month.

Listen. Then clap and practice.

George had been   thinking of   studying   Greek,

Moving to   Athens   and learning   to speak.

But he changed   his mind   and decided to   stay

With his family   and friends   and his dog   in L.A.

Jill had been   planning to   learn how to   ski,

But she tripped and   fell and   sprained   her knee.

She had been   dreaming of   mountains and   snow.

But now she's   at home and has   no place   to go.

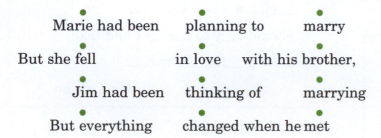

Marie had been   planning to   marry   Tim,

But she fell   in love   with his brother,   Jim.

Jim had been   thinking of   marrying   Dee,

But everything   changed when he met   Marie.

H **LISTENING**

Listen to each word and then say it.

r!

1. re<u>t</u>i<u>r</u>e
2. memo<u>r</u>ize
3. p<u>r</u>actice
4. <u>dr</u>ug s<u>t</u>o<u>r</u>e
5. favo<u>r</u>ite
6. inte<u>rr</u>upt
7. a<u>r</u>ound
8. <u>r</u>estau<u>r</u>ant

9. <u>l</u>ively
10. <u>l</u>oud<u>ly</u>
11. swo<u>ll</u>en
12. e<u>l</u>evator
13. f<u>ly</u>
14. be<u>l</u>ieve
15. co<u>l</u>d
16. fa<u>ll</u> as<u>l</u>eep

l!

1 MARYLOU'S BROKEN KEYBOARD

Marylou's keyboard is broken. The r's and the l's don't always work. Fill in the missing r's and l's, and then read Marylou's letters aloud.

1.

_R_oger,

I'm af_r_aid the__e's something w__ong with the fi__ep__ace in the __iving __oom. A__so, the __ef__ige__ato__ is b__oken. I've been ca__ing the __and__o__d fo__ th__ee days on his ce__ __ phone, but he hasn't ca__ __ed back. I hope he ca__ __s me tomo__ __ow.

Ma__y__ou

2.

__ouise,

I'm te__ __ib__y wo__ __ied about my b__othe__ La__ __y's hea__th. He hu__t his __eg whi__e he was p__aying baseba__ __. He had a__ __eady dis__ocated his shou__der whi__e he was su__fing __ast F__iday. Acco__ding to his docto__, he is a__so having p__ob__ems with his b__ood p__essu__e and with his __ight w__ist. He __ea__ __y should t__y to __e__ax and take __ife a __itt__e easie__.

Ma__y__ou

3.

A__no__d,

Can you possib__y __ecommend a good __estau__ant in you__ neighbo__hood? I'm p__anning on taking my re__atives to __unch tomo__ __ow, but I'm not su__e whe__e.

We ate at a ve__y nice G__eek __estau__ant nea__ you__ apa__tment bui__ding __ast month, but I haven't been ab__e to __emembe__ the name. Do you know the p__ace?

You__ f__iend,
Ma__y__ou

4.

__osa,

I have been p__anning a t__ip to F__o__ida. I'__ __ be f__ying to O__ __ando on F__iday, and I'__ __ be __etu__ning th__ee days __ater. Have you eve__ been the__e? I __emembe__ you had fami__y membe__s who __ived in F__o__ida seve__a__ yea__s ago.

P__ease w__ite back.

A__ __ my __ove,
Ma__y__ou

LISTENING 🔊

Listen and choose the correct answer.

1. a. He can't find it anywhere.
    b. Where can it be?
    c. Nobody can hear him. *(c circled)*

2. a. No, she isn't. She's my wife.
    b. Yes. She's my wife's cousin.
    c. No. She works for a different company.

3. a. Did you take a lot of photographs?
    b. Why did you charge it?
    c. That's too bad. You had been looking forward to it.

4. a. I know. He missed all his tests.
    b. I know. He's been doing very poorly.
    c. I know. He hasn't had a bad grade yet.

5. a. Did she find it?
    b. Whose is it?
    c. I'm sure it hurt a lot.

6. a. We stayed for the lecture.
    b. We talked about classical music.
    c. We read about psychology.

7. a. Did you enjoy yourselves?
    b. How many miles did you travel?
    c. Where did you drive?

8. a. She's having problems with her feet.
    b. She's having problems with her teeth.
    c. That's okay. We all make mistakes.

9. a. Did he make it?
    b. When did you get home?
    c. I know. He likes everything you serve.

10. a. You're right. I bought one.
    b. No, but I heard the noise.
    c. Sorry. We don't sell motorcycles.

11. a. I think so. He's been working hard.
    b. Yes. His plane will leave soon.
    c. I hope so. He never goes to work.

12. a. Poor Amy! She's always sick.
    b. Amy needs a new pair of boots.
    c. She was afraid to ask for it.

13. a. What a shame! Now she can't sing.
    b. What a shame! Now she can't knit.
    c. What a shame! Now she can't walk.

14. a. Would you like to talk about it?
    b. Who are you going to give it to?
    c. What did you decide to do?

15. a. I like you, too.
    b. What are you going to send me?
    c. You don't have anything to be jealous about.

16. a. Was it a very bad accident?
    b. Do you know anybody who can fix it?
    c. How long had they been going out?

17. a. I hope he feels better soon.
    b. What happened? Did you twist it?
    c. How are your cousins?

18. a. Did you call the doctor?
    b. What had you eaten?
    c. Why were you sad?

19. a. I'm glad to hear that.
    b. What was he angry about?
    c. What did he ask them?

20. a. We enjoyed the music.
    b. The lecture was very boring.
    c. The food was excellent.

21. a. They're too small.
    b. You have a job interview today.
    c. You have a baseball game today.

22. a. She enjoys going to the symphony.
    b. She enjoys going window-shopping.
    c. She enjoys doing gymnastics.

23. a. We're going to have a party.
    b. We're going on vacation.
    c. We received a lot of anniversary gifts.

24. a. He's glad he bought it.
    b. He's going to wear it for several years.
    c. He has to return it on Tuesday.

A. Complete the sentences with the appropriate verb form.

(eat)   **1.** Why do you keep on _____ junk food?

(wrestle)   **2.** My mother thinks _____ is dangerous.

(stop)   **3.** I've decided _____ interrupting people all the time.

(box)   **4.** Bruno practices _____ every day at the gym.

(swim)   **5.** _____ is a good way to relax.

(skate)   **6.** Where did your daughter learn _____ so well?

(talk)   **7.** Please stop _____. I'm trying to sleep!

(do)   **8.** Rita thinks that _____ exercises is a good way to start the day.

B. Complete the sentences, using the past perfect tense.

Ex. *(wear)*   I wore my favorite striped tie to work yesterday. I ___hadn't worn___ it to work in a long time.

     (start)   By the time Andrew got to the play, it ___had___ already ___started___.

(speak)   **1.** I had dinner with some Japanese friends last night. I enjoyed myself very much

         because I _____ Japanese in a long time.

(do)   **2.** By the time Jennifer's father got home from work, she _____ already

         _____ her homework, and she was ready to play baseball in the yard with him.

(leave)   **3.** Ronald was upset. By the time he got to the train, it _____ already

         _____.

(write)   **4.** I wrote an e-mail to my grandparents last night because I _____ to them for a few weeks.

(have)   **5.** Patty had pizza for lunch yesterday. She _____ pizza in a long time.

(take)   **6.** My husband and I took a walk after dinner last night. We _____ a walk after dinner in a long time.

(eat)   **7.** I ate a big piece of chocolate cake last night and felt terrible about it. I _____

         _____ a rich dessert since I started my diet.

(go)   **8.** My parents went back to their hometown last month. They _____ back there for twenty years.

C. Complete the sentences, using the past perfect continuous tense.

Ex. *(study)*   Jonathan was glad he did well on his astronomy exam. He ___had been studying___
for it for days.

(work)   **1.** Marvin didn't get his promotion at work. He was heartbroken because he

_____ overtime for several months.

(train)   **2.** I was disappointed they canceled the marathon last week. I _____

_____ for it since last summer.

(argue)   **3.** Jane and John broke up last night. They _____
with each other for the past several weeks.

(plan)   **4.** Nancy caught a cold and couldn't go on her camping trip. It's a shame because she

_____ it since last April.

D. Listen and choose the correct answer.

Ex. (a.) go fishing.
   b. going canoeing.

1. a. tease her little brother.
   b. interrupting people.

2. a. moving to Miami.
   b. to sell our house.

3. a. to buy a sports car.
   b. buying a sports car.

4. a. waiting in line.
   b. drive downtown.

5. a. going out with Richard.
   b. ask for a raise.

Read the article on student book page 111 and answer the questions.

SIDE by SIDE Gazette

STUDENT BOOK
PAGES **111–114**

1. The 1988 Winter Olympic Games were in
   ____.
   a. Jamaica
   b. Canada
   c. Lake Placid, New York
   d. Norway

2. People were surprised that ____.
   a. Jamaica had a bobsled team
   b. the Jamaican team had poor equipment
   c. the Jamaican team didn't do well
   d. the Jamaican team had trained hard

3. You can infer that most of the Jamaican athletes saw snow for the first time in
   ____.
   a. Jamaica
   b. Calgary
   c. Lake Placid
   d. Germany

4. In the third paragraph, *give up* means
   ____.
   a. quit
   b. win
   c. compete
   d. go home

5. To prepare for the 1988 Winter Olympics, the team ____ in Jamaica.
   a. practiced skiing
   b. ran and lifted weights
   c. rode their bobsled
   d. made a movie

6. In 1993 ____.
   a. the Jamaican team did the impossible
   b. the team went back to Calgary
   c. the team arrived in Norway
   d. many people saw a movie about the team

7. In 1994, the Jamaican team came in ____.
   a. tenth in a four-person bobsled
   b. second in a ten-person bobsled
   c. tenth in a two-person bobsled
   d. fourteenth in a two-person bobsled

8. The Jamaican team won the hearts of fans around the world because ____.
   a. they were movie stars
   b. they had done something difficult and unusual
   c. people like Jamaican music
   d. they had won the Olympics

9. The purpose of this article is ____.
   a. to compare Winter and Summer Olympics
   b. to describe Olympic training centers
   c. to explain why Jamaican music is popular
   d. to tell the story of an interesting team of athletes

10. In the bottom left caption under the team's photograph, *part fact and part fiction* means ____.
    a. some parts of the movie are true
    b. some actors in the movie are athletes
    c. they made the movie in Jamaica
    d. they didn't make the movie in Jamaica

B FACT FILE

Look at the Fact File on student book page 113 and answer the questions.

1. ____ countries competed in the Olympics in 1952.
   a. More than one hundred
   b. More than fifty
   c. More than ninety
   d. Between eighty and one hundred

2. About twice as many countries competed in 2000 as in ____.
   a. 1900
   b. 1924
   c. 1952
   d. 1976

C INTERVIEW

Read the interview on student book page 112 and answer the questions.

1. Olga ____ when she was four years old.
   a. moved
   b. had a coach
   c. prepared for a competition
   d. started to skate

2. Olga has been living in the United States ____.
   a. for ten years
   b. since she was seven years old
   c. since she was ten years old
   d. since she met Mr. Abrams

3. Olga won her first medal ____.
   a. seven years ago
   b. before her seventh birthday
   c. after she started to take lessons with Mr. Abrams
   d. after the Regional Competition

4. Olga doesn't take lessons at a skating program in her city because ____.
   a. she doesn't like the teachers
   b. she doesn't like the schedule
   c. she doesn't have time
   d. she has finished all the levels

5. Three months after this interview, Olga is going to compete in the ____.
   a. Regional Figure Skating Competition
   b. National Competition
   c. Summer Olympics
   d. Winter Olympics

6. To prepare for the Regional Figure Skating Competition, Olga trained ____.
   a. seven hours a day
   b. eight hours a day
   c. nine hours a day
   d. ten hours a day

7. When Olga won the Regional Competition, she competed against ____.
   a. women from her part of the country
   b. men and women from her city
   c. women from other countries
   d. women from other parts of the country

8. If Olga does poorly in the National Competition, she ____ in the Olympics next winter.
   a. has to compete
   b. might compete
   c. can't compete
   d. is going to compete

9. When Olga talks about practicing her *routines* over and over again, she is referring to ____.
   a. getting up early
   b. the dances she performs on the ice
   c. her exercises
   d. her medals

10. *Over and over* means ____.
    a. many times
    b. up and down
    c. quickly
    d. slowly

D YOU'RE THE INTERVIEWER!

Imagine you are interviewing a famous athlete! Ask these questions, do some research on the Internet to find the answers, and write the answers below. Then share what you learned with the class.

When did you begin to (play _____, compete in _____)?	
What kind of training do you do?	
What was your best game/competition? Why? How had you prepared for it?	

E FUN WITH IDIOMS: What's the Meaning?

Match the expressions and words.

1. Break a ____!

2. Get off my ____!

3. Hold your ____!

4. Keep your ____ up!

5. Put your best ____ forward!

6. Keep your ____ on the ball!

back	Be quiet!
chin	Don't be sad!
leg	Don't bother me!
tongue	Pay attention!
eye	Try hard!
foot	Good luck!

F FUN WITH IDIOMS: Finish the Conversations

Choose the correct expression to complete each conversation.

1. A. I can't believe I made such a stupid mistake!

   B. You weren't paying attention. Keep your eye on the ball / Keep your chin up , and it won't happen again.

2. A. I can't stand Mr. Roberts, our math teacher.

   B. Break a leg! / Hold your tongue! Here he comes!

3. A. I'm so upset. My husband just lost his job.

   B. Don't worry. Keep your chin up! / Put your best foot forward! I'm sure he'll find a new job soon.

4. A. You watch TV all the time, and you never clean your room!

   B. Keep your eye on the ball / Get off my back , Charlie! Maybe you should look for a new roommate!

5. A. The play is beginning. I hope I don't forget my lines.

   B. Hold your tongue! / Break a leg!

   A. Thanks.

6. A. Tomorrow is the gymnastics competition. I'm a little nervous.

   B. Get off my back! / Put your best foot forward! I'm sure you'll be fine.

WE'VE GOT MAIL!

Choose the words that best complete each sentence.

1. Maria _____ to drive.
   a. enjoys
   b. avoids
   c. hates
   d. practices

2. I'm thinking about _____.
   a. get marrying
   b. to get married
   c. getting to marry
   d. getting married

3. I decided _____.
   a. going back to college
   b. to look for a new apartment
   c. time to move to Miami
   d. will start my own business

4. By the time I got to the movie, it _____.
   a. has already started
   b. is already beginning
   c. had already began
   d. had already started

5. I didn't take a vacation in July. I _____ a vacation the month before.
   a. have already been taking
   b. have already taken
   c. had already taken
   d. had already took

6. When my husband got home, I _____ dinner.
   a. had already eaten
   b. already eaten
   c. have already eaten
   d. already eating

Choose the sentence that is correct and complete.

7. a. I'm learning speaking English.
   b. I'm learning to understand English.
   c. I'm learning read English.
   d. I'm learning to writing English.

8. a. He kept on talk all night.
   b. He kept on talking all night.
   c. He kept on to talk all night.
   d. He kept on to talking all night.

9. a. I enjoy to swim at the beach.
   b. I enjoy go swimming at the beach.
   c. I enjoy to go swimming at the beach.
   d. I enjoy swimming at the beach.

10. a. They hadn't went there before.
    b. They didn't went there before.
    c. They hadn't gone there before.
    d. They haven't went there before.

"CAN-DO" REVIEW

Match the "can do" statement and the correct sentence.

_____ 1. I can introduce myself.

_____ 2. I can agree with someone.

_____ 3. I can describe my feelings and emotions.

_____ 4. I can express appreciation.

_____ 5. I can offer advice.

_____ 6. I can describe an accomplishment.

_____ 7. I can describe forgetting to do something.

_____ 8. I can react to bad news.

_____ 9. I can ask if someone agrees.

_____ 10. I can report household repair problems.

a. That's very nice of you.

b. Our water heater hasn't been working.

c. I passed my driver's test yesterday.

d. You're right.

e. Don't you think so?

f. That's terrible!

g. Hi. My name is Daniel.

h. I think you should start your own business.

i. I'm nervous.

j. I had forgotten to turn off my computer.

9

1. A. Did you pick up Rover at the vet?

    B. No. I didn't _____pick him up_____.
        I thought YOU did.

2. A. Did you turn on the heat?

    B. Yes. I _____ a few
        hours ago, but it's still cold in here.

3. A. You should take back these library
        books.

    B. I know. I'll _____
        tomorrow morning.

4. A. Has Diane filled out her income tax
        forms?

    B. No. She's going to _____
        this weekend.

5. A. Where should we hang up this
        portrait?

    B. Let's _____
        over the fireplace.

6. A. I'm having trouble hooking up my
        computer.

    B. No problem. I'll _____.

7. A. Are you ever going to throw out these
        old souvenirs?

    B. I'll _____
        some day.

8. A. Did Sally take back her cell phone to
        the store?

    B. Yes. She _____
        this afternoon.

9. A. Did your daughter take down the
        photographs of her old boyfriend?

    B. Yes. She _____
        as soon as they stopped going out.

10. A. Did you remember to call up Aunt
         Clara to wish her "Happy Birthday"?

     B. Sorry. I didn't _____.
         I forgot it was her birthday.

| bring back | hand in | put away | put on | take off | turn off | turn on | wake up |

1. I think we should __turn on__ the air conditioner. It's getting very hot in here.

   Good idea. I'll _____ right away.

2. When are you going to __hand__ your biology report __in__?

   I'm going to _____ tomorrow morning. I have to write it tonight.

3. Let's _____ Mom and Dad! It's 8:00, and they're still sleeping!

   Don't _____. It's Saturday. They don't go to work today.

4. Don't forget to _____ the printer _____ before you leave the office tonight.

   You don't have to worry. I always _____ before I leave.

5. Why don't you _____ your hat and coat? It's warm in here.

   I'll _____ in a few minutes. I'm still a little cold.

6. Susie, when are you going to _____ your toys _____?

   I'm still playing with them. I'll _____ later.

7. Teddy, it's time for bed. _____ your pajamas _____!

   Okay, Dad. I'll _____ in a few minutes.

8. Do you think Richard will _____ his girlfriend _____ to the house after the dance?

   I don't know. Maybe he'll _____. I hope he does. I really want to meet her.

Listen. Then clap and practice.

A.   Take off your   skis.
      Take them off   now!

B.   I can't take them   off.
      I don't know   how!

A.   Turn off the   engine!
      Turn it off   now!

B.   I can't turn it   off.
      I don't know   how!

A.   Turn on the   oven!
      Turn it on   now!

B.   I can't turn it   on.
      I don't know   how!

A.   Hook up the   printer!
      Hook it up   now!

B.   I can't hook it   up.
      I don't know   how!

A.   Pick up the   suitcase.
      Give it to   Jack.

B.   I can't pick it   up.
      I have   a bad back!

A.   Take back   the videos!
      Take them back today.

B.   I can't take them   back.
      It's a holiday!

WHAT ARE THEY SAYING?

cross out	give back	look up	throw away	turn off
do over	hook up	think over	turn down	write down

1. *Did your teacher like the composition you wrote about Australian birds?*

   No, she didn't. I have to _do it over_ .

2. A. Do we still have the hammer we borrowed from our next-door neighbors?

   B. No, we don't. We _____ a long time ago.

3. A. What's the matter with the answering machine? Is it broken?

   B. No, it isn't. I forgot to _____.

4. A. Are you going to accept the invitation to Roger's wedding?

   B. I don't know. I have to _____ carefully. His wedding is in Alaska.

5. A. What's the weather forecast for tomorrow?

   B. I'm not sure. You should _____ on the Internet.

6. A. Is Kimberly going to the prom with Frank?

   B. No, she isn't. She had to _____ because she already had a date with somebody else.

7. A. What should I do with all these letters from my ex-boyfriend?

   B. I think you should _____.

8. A. What's Walter's new address?

   B. I can't remember. But I know I've _____ somewhere.

9. A. Should I erase all these mistakes in my math homework?

   B. No, I think you should just _____.

10. *Why aren't you watching the president's speech on TV?*

    I watched it for a while, but it was boring. So I _____.

James just moved into a new apartment. What does he have to do?

1. He has to (put away) / throw away his books and his clothes.

2. He has to fill out / hook up his printer and his computer.

3. He has to take out / take back the moving truck he rented.

Jennifer is very happy and excited. She just got engaged. What's she going to do?

4. She's going to wake up / drop off her parents and tell them the news.

5. She's going to call off / call up all her friends.

6. She's going to look up / write down all the things her boyfriend said.

Mr. and Mrs. Baker's aunt and uncle are going to visit them next week. What do the Bakers have to do before then?

7. They have to clean up / take out their apartment.

8. They have to pick out / put away their children's toys.

9. They have to throw out / hook up all their old newspapers.

10. They have to call up / hang up their aunt and uncle's portrait.

F WHAT SHOULD THEY DO?

| figure out | look up | throw out | use up |
| give back | think over | turn off | wake up |

1. Abigail, will you marry me?

That's a big decision, Howard. I have to _____think it *over*_____.

2. A. I've been using my neighbor's screwdriver all summer.

    B. Don't you think it's time to _____?

3. A. Is there any more sugar?

    B. No. We _____. We have to buy some tomorrow.

4. A. I don't know the definition of this word.

    B. You really should _____ in the dictionary.

5. A. This math problem is very difficult.

    B. Maybe your mother can help you _____.

6. A. It's 7:30, and the children are still sleeping.

    B. They're going to be late for school. I'll _____.

7. A. It's really cold in here! Is the air conditioner on?

    B. Yes, it is. I'll _____ right away.

8. A. I'm very embarrassed. These are the worst photographs anyone has ever taken of me.

    B. Well, if they bother you that much, why don't you _____?

G LISTENING

Listen and choose the correct answer.

1. a. picked it up.
    (b.) used it up.

2. a. turn it down.
    b. turn it on.

3. a. take them down.
    b. turn them down.

4. a. think them over.
    b. drop them off.

5. a. hook it up.
    b. look it up.

6. a. give it back?
    b. hand it in?

7. a. throw it out.
    b. figure it out.

8. a. write it down.
    b. use it up.

9. a. pick it up.
    b. clean it up.

Activity Workbook **105**

COME UP WITH THE RIGHT ANSWER

call on	get over	look through	pick on	take after
get along with	hear from	look up to	run into	

1. I ___take after___ my father. We're both athletic, we're both interested in engineering, and we both like to paint. I'm really

   glad I ___take after him___.

2. I haven't _____ my son in three weeks. He's

   at college, and I usually _____ every week!

3. I'm so embarrassed. My teacher _____ me twice in class today, but I didn't know ANY of the answers. I have to study

   tonight. She might _____ again tomorrow.

4. My husband and I enjoyed _____ our wedding

   pictures. We hadn't _____ in years.

5. Jack _____ his cold very quickly. I think he

   _____ fast because he stayed home and took care of himself.

6. I really _____ my grandmother. She's honest, she's intelligent, and she's very generous. I hope someday when I'm a

   grandmother, my grandchildren will _____, too.

7. I was very surprised. I _____ my old girlfriend at the

   bank yesterday morning. And then I _____ again at a movie last night.

8. I don't _____ my mother-in-law. We often

   disagree. All the people in our family _____.
   Why can't I?

9. Bobby is mean. He _____ his cats all the time.

   The cats don't like it when Bobby _____.

GRAMMARRAP: *I Don't Get Along with Kate and Clem*

Listen. Then clap and practice.

I don't   get along with   Kate and   Clem.

I almost   never   hear from   them.

But I get along   well   with Bob   and Fay.

I call them   up   three times   a day.

Jack   takes after   his Uncle   Jim.

Bob   looks up to   his father,   Tim.

Kate never   picks on   her sister,   Sue.

But she always   picks on   her brother,   Lou.

J **CHOOSE**

1. A. Do we have any more pens?
   B. No, we don't. We _____.
      a. ran into them
      (b.) ran out of them

2. A. Does Carol still have the flu?
   B. No. She _____ a few days ago.
      a. got over it
      b. got it over

3. A. Does Jill get along with her brother?
   B. No. He _____ all the time.
      a. picks her on
      b. picks on her

4. A. I can't remember Tom's phone number.
   B. You should _____.
      a. look up to him
      b. look it up

5. A. Amy knows all the answers in class.
   B. Does the teacher always _____?
      a. call on her
      b. call her on

6. A. This is a very difficult problem.
   B. I know. I can't _____.
      a. figure out it
      b. figure it out

7. A. Have you heard from Pam recently?
   B. Yes. I _____ the other day.
      a. heard her from
      b. heard from her

8. A. What should I do with these old letters?
   B. Why don't you _____?
      a. throw them out
      b. throw out them

9. A. These photographs are wonderful!
   B. I know. Let's _____ again.
      a. look through them
      b. look them through

10. A. Do you like William?
    B. Oh, yes. I _____ very well.
       a. get him along
       b. get along with him

11. A. Should I turn off the computer?
    B. No. You can _____.
       a. leave it on
       b. leave on it

12. A. Did you hang up your uncle's portrait?
    B. No, I didn't. I _____.
       a. took it down
       b. took down it

13. A. You look like your father.
    B. I know. Everybody says I _____.
       a. take him after
       b. take after him

14. A. They have a very unusual last name.
    B. You'll remember it if you _____.
       a. write down it
       b. write it down

WHAT DOES IT MEAN?

Choose the correct answer.

1. Richard takes after his mother.
   a. He's always with her.
   (b.) They're both shy.
   c. His mother always arrives first.

2. Please turn off the air conditioner.
   a. It's too hot in this room.
   b. The room is too small.
   c. It's too cold in this room.

3. Tom left his briefcase on the plane.
   a. Maybe his mind slipped.
   b. He forgot it.
   c. He was very careful.

4. I'm going to take these pants back.
   a. They're new.
   b. They're medium.
   c. They're too baggy.

5. Fran can't find her notebook.
   a. I hope she didn't throw it out.
   b. I hope she didn't fill it out.
   c. I hope she didn't take it off.

6. Bob doesn't get along with his neighbors.
   a. He can't stand to talk to them.
   b. He likes them very much.
   c. He looks up to them.

7. I hope I don't run into my old boyfriend.
   a. Why? Will he get hurt?
   b. Why don't you want to see him?
   c. Why? Does he like to jog?

8. Paul had to do his homework over.
   a. It was excellent.
   b. He didn't think it over.
   c. He had made a lot of mistakes.

L **LISTENING**

Listen and choose the correct answer.

1. a. He's very tall.
   b. I can never find him.
   (c.) I want to be like him.

2. a. You're lucky he has a car.
   b. I'm sure that bothers you.
   c. Do you also pick him up?

3. a. Yes. I put it in the closet.
   b. Yes. I gave it to our neighbor.
   c. Yes. We had used it all up.

4. a. I'm sorry you're still sick.
   b. I'm glad you're feeling better.
   c. It's too bad you have to do it over.

5. a. No. He speaks very softly.
   b. Yes. He sent me an e-mail yesterday.
   c. No. I haven't heard him recently.

6. a. The music was very loud.
   b. Somebody had picked it up.
   c. I already had another date.

7. a. Yes, several times.
   b. Yes, but I wasn't home.
   c. Yes, but I had already left the house.

8. a. He didn't need it anymore.
   b. It was already at the cleaner's.
   c. I know. He found one he really liked.

9. a. Did she hurt herself?
   b. How did you hurt yourself?
   c. When does her plane leave?

10. a. The store isn't having a sale.
    b. Everything in the store is cheaper.
    c. Everything is 20 cents less this week.

11. a. Good. I'll buy it.
    b. Don't worry. We have larger ones.
    c. I know. It's too tight.

12. a. Yes. I used up four pair.
    b. Yes. I put on four pair.
    c. Yes. I looked up four pair.

1. I ate too much. So _____did I_____.

2. I hate to go to the mall. _____, too.

3. I can play the trombone. So _____.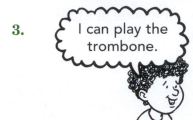

4. I'm allergic to milk. _____, too.

5. I'll be starting college this fall. _____, too.

6. I was late for work. So _____.

7. I'm going to retire soon. So _____.

8. I've been doing poorly in school recently. _____, too.

9. I just got a promotion. _____, too.

10. I'll be on vacation next week. So _____.

11. I have to lose a little weight.  So _____.

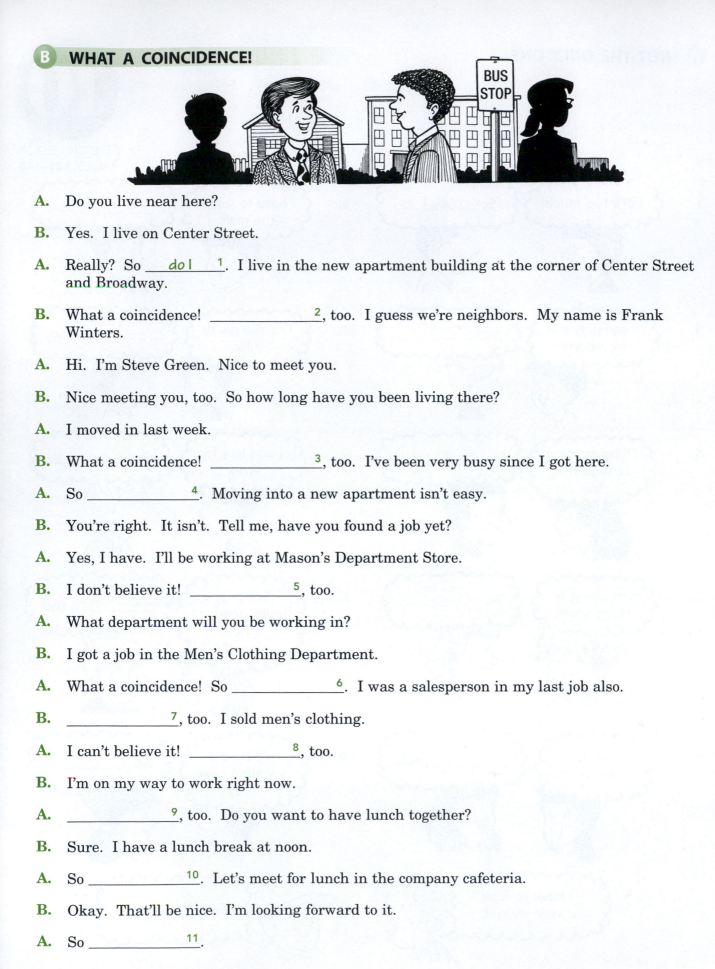

A. Do you live near here?

B. Yes. I live on Center Street.

A. Really? So ____do I____ ¹. I live in the new apartment building at the corner of Center Street and Broadway.

B. What a coincidence! _____², too. I guess we're neighbors. My name is Frank Winters.

A. Hi. I'm Steve Green. Nice to meet you.

B. Nice meeting you, too. So how long have you been living there?

A. I moved in last week.

B. What a coincidence! _____³, too. I've been very busy since I got here.

A. So _____⁴. Moving into a new apartment isn't easy.

B. You're right. It isn't. Tell me, have you found a job yet?

A. Yes, I have. I'll be working at Mason's Department Store.

B. I don't believe it! _____⁵, too.

A. What department will you be working in?

B. I got a job in the Men's Clothing Department.

A. What a coincidence! So _____⁶. I was a salesperson in my last job also.

B. _____⁷, too. I sold men's clothing.

A. I can't believe it! _____⁸, too.

B. I'm on my way to work right now.

A. _____⁹, too. Do you want to have lunch together?

B. Sure. I have a lunch break at noon.

A. So _____¹⁰. Let's meet for lunch in the company cafeteria.

B. Okay. That'll be nice. I'm looking forward to it.

A. So _____¹¹.

1. I didn't like the movie.
   Neither ___did I___.

2. I'm not feeling very well.
   _____ either.

3. I wasn't in school yesterday.
   Neither _____.

4. I can't play tennis very well.
   _____ either.

5. I won't be home tonight.
   _____ either.

6. I've never been in the hospital before.
   Neither _____.

7. I can't stand driving in traffic.
   _____ either.

8. I'm not going to order dessert.
   Neither _____.

9. I didn't enjoy the lecture.
   _____ either.

10. I don't like to practice the piano.
    Neither _____.

11. I'll never go sailing again.
    Neither _____.

D LISTENING

Listen and complete the sentences.

1. So _____did I_____.

2. _____, too.

3. So _____.

4. _____ either.

5. _____, too.

6. _____, too.

7. Neither _____.

8. _____, too.

9. Neither _____.

10. So _____.

11. _____ either.

12. _____, too.

13. Neither _____.

14. So _____.

15. _____ either.

E GRAMMARRAP: *So Do I*

Listen. Then clap and practice.

A. I like to   fly.

B. So do   I.

A. They like to   ski.

B. So do   we.

A. She likes the   zoo.

B. He does,   too.

A. You're a good   friend.

B. So are   you.

F GRAMMARRAP: *They Didn't Either*

Listen. Then clap and practice.

We didn't   eat it.

They didn't   either.

He didn't   finish it.

Neither did   she.

She wasn't   hungry.

He wasn't   either.

They weren't   hungry.

Neither were   we.

WHAT ARE THEY SAYING?

1. Why were you and your brother late for school today?

   I had to go to the dentist, and so _____*did he*_____.

2. Will you and your wife be home this evening?

   I don't think so. I'll be working late, and so _____.

3. How did you and Tom feel after you ran in the marathon?

   I was exhausted, and _____, too.

4. Would you and your sister like to learn how to ski?

   Actually, I've already tried it, and so _____.

5. Can Ricky and I go to the movies tonight?

   He should study for his English exam, and _____, too.

6. Have you seen Mr. and Mrs. Martinez recently?

   I saw them today. I was in the park, and _____, too.

7. Should I go into the water with Timmy and Susie?

   No. That's okay. Timmy can swim, and _____ Susie.

8. Why weren't you and your brother at baseball practice today?

   I had to help my mother, and so _____.

9. Why are you and your wife leaving the party?

   She has to get up early tomorrow, and _____, too.

10. Why are your parents so worried?

    I've decided to ...., and .... my brother.

H WHAT ARE THEY SAYING?

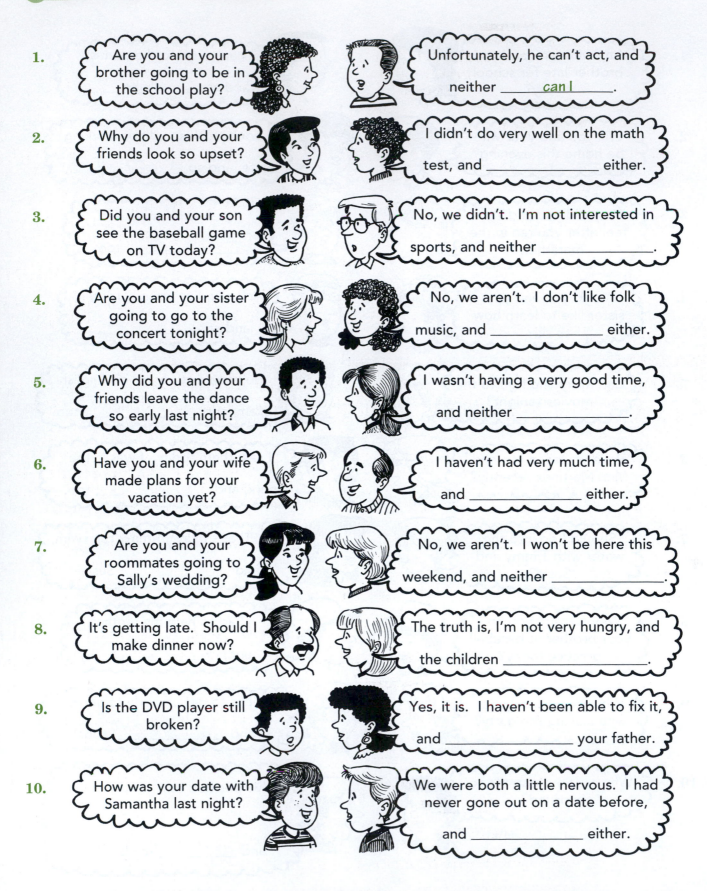

1. Are you and your brother going to be in the school play?

   Unfortunately, he can't act, and neither _____can I_____.

2. Why do you and your friends look so upset?

   I didn't do very well on the math test, and _____ either.

3. Did you and your son see the baseball game on TV today?

   No, we didn't. I'm not interested in sports, and neither _____.

4. Are you and your sister going to go to the concert tonight?

   No, we aren't. I don't like folk music, and _____ either.

5. Why did you and your friends leave the dance so early last night?

   I wasn't having a very good time, and neither _____.

6. Have you and your wife made plans for your vacation yet?

   I haven't had very much time, and _____ either.

7. Are you and your roommates going to Sally's wedding?

   No, we aren't. I won't be here this weekend, and neither _____.

8. It's getting late. Should I make dinner now?

   The truth is, I'm not very hungry, and the children _____.

9. Is the DVD player still broken?

   Yes, it is. I haven't been able to fix it, and _____ your father.

10. How was your date with Samantha last night?

    We were both a little nervous. I had never gone out on a date before, and _____ either.

WHAT ARE THEY SAYING?

so	too	either	neither

1. A. Why didn't Ronald and his wife go to work yesterday?

   B. He had a terrible cold,

   and { ___*so did she*___.
   ___*she did, too*___. }

2. A. Did Betty and Bob enjoy the concert last night?

   B. Not really. She couldn't hear the music,

   and { _____.
   _____. }

3. A. Do Jack and his girlfriend enjoy going sailing?

   B. No, they don't. She gets seasick,

   and { _____.
   _____. }

4. A. Why didn't Mr. and Mrs. Miller order the cheesecake for dessert?

   B. He doesn't eat rich foods,

   and { _____.
   _____. }

5. A. Why did Beverly and Brian have trouble doing their chemistry experiments?

   B. He hadn't followed the instructions,

   and { _____.
   _____. }

6. A. Why aren't you and Peter good friends any more?

   B. I'm in love with Amanda Richardson,

   and { _____.
   _____. }

1. I'm tall, but my sister and brother _____*aren't*_____ . I've always _____ the tallest person in our family.

2. My brother isn't very athletic, but my sister _____ . She enjoys _____ squash and _____ gymnastics.

3. I can't draw pictures, but my brother _____ . He's been _____ pictures since he _____ four years old.

4. My brother and I have different interests. I enjoy seeing movies, but my brother _____ . He enjoys _____ to lectures and concerts.

5. My mother is interested in photography, but my father _____ . My mother _____ photographs since she was a teenager.

6. My father has lived here all his life, but his parents _____ . They've _____ in this country _____ fifty years. Before that, they _____ in Italy.

7. My grandparents sometimes speak to us in Italian, but my father _____ . He _____ Italian to anyone in a long time.

8. I'll be going to college next year, but my brother _____ . He _____ finished high school yet.

9. I don't have a very good voice, but my sister _____ . She sings in the school choir. She has _____ in the choir _____ she started high school.

10. I'm usually very neat, but my sister and brother _____ . They never hang _____ their clothes or put _____ their books.

11. I know how to ski, but my brother _____ . I've been skiing _____ the past nine years.

12. My sister is a very good skater, but my brother and I _____ . We just started _____ a month ago. Before that, we _____ never _____ at all.

Listen and complete the sentences.

1. but my husband _____ didn't _____.

2. but my daughter _____.

3. but you _____.

4. but I _____.

5. but my friends _____.

6. but my wife _____.

7. but you _____.

8. but my brother _____.

9. but everybody else _____.

10. but our teacher _____.

11. but my son _____.

12. but the other man _____.

13. but my sister _____.

14. but I _____.

15. but my friends _____.

16. but my brother _____.

17. but my children _____.

18. but I _____.

L GRAMMARRAP: *I've Been Working Hard, and You Have, Too* 🔊

Listen. Then clap and practice.

I've been working hard, and   you have,   too.

I'm   exhausted,   and so   are you.

He's been   out of town,   and so   has she.

They've been very   busy,   and so   have we.

I   didn't go,   and neither   did he.

They   weren't there,   and neither   were we.

We   stayed home,   and so   did they.

Nobody   went   to the meeting   that day.

I don't speak   Greek,   but my brother   does.

I wasn't born in   Greece,   but my mother   was.

I didn't study   Greek,   but my brother   did.

He's spoken   Greek   since he was   a kid.

SOUND IT OUT! 🔊))

Listen to each word and then say it.

f**u**ll		f**oo**l	
1. l**oo**k	3. p**u**t	1. n**oo**n	3. J**u**dy
2. c**ou**ld	4. f**oo**t	2. dr**ew**	4. f**oo**d

Listen and put a circle around the word that has the same sound.

1. f**u**ll: p**oo**l   (c**oo**ks)   sh**oe**

2. fl**u**:   t**oo**   w**ou**ld   bl**oo**d

3. g**oo**d: s**ou**p   sh**ou**ldn't   J**u**ne

4. w**oo**d: fl**u**   t**oo**th   p**u**t

5. c**ou**ld: c**u**p   c**oo**kies   **u**pstairs

6. h**oo**k: f**oo**d   m**o**vie   g**oo**d

7. w**o**man: s**u**gar   tr**ue**   n**ew**

Now make a sentence using all the words you circled, and read the sentence aloud.

8. .... much ....
   in their ....

9. s**ui**t: tw**o**   p**u**t   b**u**s

10. c**oo**k: f**oo**d   b**oo**ks   s**u**nny

11. f**oo**t: b**oo**kcase   p**oo**l   m**u**st

12. bl**ue**:   j**u**st   wh**o**   l**oo**ked

13. w**ou**ld: s**ui**t   t**oo**l   t**oo**k

14. c**oo**l: st**oo**d   aftern**oo**n   p**u**lse

15. sch**oo**l: S**u**san's   th**u**nder   fl**oo**r

Now make a sentence using all the words you circled, and read the sentence aloud.

16. .... from ....
    .... this ....?

__j__	1.	afford	a.	afraid
_____	2.	argue	b.	do poorly
_____	3.	bachelor	c.	fight
_____	4.	begin	d.	finish
_____	5.	bump into	e.	friendly and talkative
_____	6.	can't stand	f.	give back
_____	7.	compatible	g.	give lessons
_____	8.	consider	h.	hate
_____	9.	continue	i.	have a lot in common
_____	10.	discuss	j.	have enough money
_____	11.	exam	k.	how much it costs
_____	12.	exhausted	l.	hurt
_____	13.	fail	m.	keep on
_____	14.	frightened	n.	meet
_____	15.	hike	o.	ready
_____	16.	injure	p.	recently
_____	17.	lately	q.	single man
_____	18.	outgoing	r.	someone who doesn't eat meat
_____	19.	prepared	s.	start
_____	20.	price	t.	study again
_____	21.	return	u.	take a long walk
_____	22.	review	v.	talk about
_____	23.	stand in line	w.	test
_____	24.	teach	x.	think about
_____	25.	use up	y.	tired
_____	26.	vegetarian	z.	wait

A. Complete the sentences.

Ex. My son is waiting for me at the bus stop. I have to pick ___him___ ___up___ right away.

My mother and I are both tall with curly hair. Everybody says I take ___after___ ___her___.

1. I'll finish my homework in a little while, and then I'll hand _____ _____.

2. My father is a very smart man. I really look _____ _____ _____.

3. I haven't talked to Aunt Shirley lately. I hope I hear _____ _____ soon.

4. My English teacher didn't like my composition. I have to do _____ _____.

5. I don't know the definition of this word. I need to look _____ _____.

6. I can't find any flour. I think we ran _____ _____ _____.

7. I can't find my wallet. Could you help me look _____ _____?

8. Don't leave your clothes on the bed. You really should hang _____ _____.

9. Don't worry about your mistakes. You can always cross _____ _____.

10. I can never remember Alan's address. I should write _____ _____.

11. I've had the flu for the past several days. My doctor says I'll get _____ _____ soon.

B. Complete the sentences.

so	too	neither	either

Ex. Maria did well on her science test, and _____so did_____ her sister.

1. I'm wearing new shoes today, and _____ my brother.

2. I won't be able to come to the meeting tomorrow, and _____ Barbara.

3. I was bored during Professor Gray's lecture, and my friends _____.

4. Janet can't skate, and her brother _____.

5. I've been taking guitar lessons for years, and _____ my sisters.

6. David worked overtime yesterday, and his wife _____.

7. Louise has never been to Europe, and _____ her husband.

8. I want to complain to the landlord, and _____ my neighbors.

9. I'm not very athletic, and _____ my wife.

● **120   Activity Workbook**

C. Listen and complete the sentences.

Ex. but her husband ____doesn't____.

1. but my sister _____.

2. but my parents _____.

3. but my brother _____.

4. but my wife _____.

5. but I _____.

A FROM MATCHMAKERS TO DATING SERVICES

Read the article on student book page 145 and answer the questions.

1. In a traditional Indian family, _____.
   a. the mother finds a husband for her daughter
   b. the father finds a husband for his daughter
   c. the daughter finds her own husband
   d. a matchmaker finds a husband for the daughter

2. A traditional Indian family wants their daughter to marry a man who _____.
   a. has a good job
   b. is an astrologer
   c. met their daughter at school
   d. reads horoscopes

3. Families hire astrologers to _____.
   a. find out when their child was born
   b. introduce young people to each other
   c. predict if a young man and woman are good for each other
   d. arrange a marriage

4. An astrologer approves a match if the man and woman _____.
   a. fall in love
   b. have the same interests
   c. have good occupations
   d. have birth dates and times that are a good match

5. People who use dating services probably don't _____.
   a. answer questions about their interests
   b. submit a photograph
   c. submit a horoscope
   d. answer questions about their education

6. In the fourth paragraph, *submit* means to _____.
   a. buy   c. take
   b. copy   d. send in

7. Many young people put personal ads in newspapers because _____.
   a. it's a family tradition
   b. they want to meet someone
   c. they want to hire a matchmaker
   d. they want to save money

8. You can infer that marriages that parents arrange _____.
   a. are becoming less common
   b. are happier than other marriages
   c. don't last as long as other marriages
   d. are more common in cities than in rural areas

9. The purpose of this article is _____.
   a. to recommend ways to meet people
   b. to give advice to young people
   c. to describe traditions and customs in different parts of the world
   d. to warn about matchmakers and astrologers

10. A key detail that supports the main idea of the article is _____.
   a. astrologers in India read a young man's horoscope to decide if there is a good match
   b. dating services are more popular than before
   c. matchmakers are common in rural areas
   d. some parents arrange marriages before children are born

B FACT FILE

Look at the Fact File on student book page 145 and answer the questions.

1. Women in Japan usually get married _____ than women in Mexico.
   a. four years later   c. six years later
   b. five years later   d. seven years later

2. Women in Swaziland usually get married 12 years earlier than women in _____.
   a. Saudi Arabia   c. Japan
   b. Australia   d. Sweden

AROUND THE WORLD

Read the article on student book page 146 and answer the questions.

1. Brides often wear _____ on their heads.
   a. a bouquet
   b. confetti
   c. a veil
   d. a helmet

2. A _____ is NOT a place of worship.
   a. mosque
   b. reception hall
   c. temple
   d. church

3. A public wedding _____.
   a. is always outdoors
   b. is very short
   c. doesn't have many guests
   d. is for everybody in the neighborhood

4. The groom in the Hindu ceremony is wearing _____.
   a. a veil
   b. a crown
   c. a bowtie
   d. a tuxedo

5. People do NOT shower the bride and groom with _____ for good luck.
   a. confetti
   b. flower petals
   c. water
   d. rice

6. A wedding procession is _____.
   a. a parade
   b. wedding music
   c. a traditional dance
   d. a special food

7. In Cyprus, _____.
   a. the guests throw money at the bride and groom
   b. the bride and groom give the guests money
   c. the bride gives money to the groom
   d. the guests attach money to the bride and groom's clothes

8. The bride and groom in Colombia _____.
   a. are putting candles in a cake
   b. are lighting candles
   c. are making a wish
   d. are singing a song

9. In the United States, the bride throws _____.
   a. rice
   b. confetti
   c. a bouquet
   d. flower petals

10. According to tradition, the person who catches the bouquet will _____.
    a. have good luck
    b. light a candle
    c. cut the cake
    d. get married next

D **INTERVIEW**

Read the Interviews on student book page 147 and answer the questions.

1. The couple who paid to meet each other met _____.
   a. at a bookstore
   b. at work
   c. through a dating service
   d. in college

2. *High school sweethearts* are _____.
   a. high school friends
   b. high school classmates
   c. high school teammates
   d. a boyfriend and girlfriend in high school

3. The youngest couple to start going out together was probably the couple who _____.
   a. met through a dating service
   b. were high school sweethearts
   c. met at work
   d. met in college

4. On a *blind date,* _____.
   a. you wear a mask
   b. you close your eyes
   c. you go out with someone you have never met before
   d. you talk on the telephone

E FUN WITH IDIOMS

Choose the best response.

1. George gave me the cold shoulder.
   a. Did you see a doctor?
   b. I'm surprised. I thought he liked you.
   c. What are you going to give him?
   d. That's nice.

2. I'm nuts about Sally.
   a. I don't like her either.
   b. You shouldn't be angry at her.
   c. What's wrong with her?
   d. You should tell her. I think she likes you, too.

3. Rosa stood me up.
   a. There weren't any seats left.
   b. She's very helpful.
   c. Maybe she had to work late.
   d. Did you enjoy your date?

4. I fell for Harry the moment I met him.
   a. Really? So quickly?
   b. What a terrible way to meet someone!
   c. When did you start to like him?
   d. He's very clumsy.

F WE'VE GOT MAIL!

Choose the words that best complete each sentence.

1. Wake _____ at 8:00.
   a. up me
   b. up him
   c. up them
   d. up your sister

2. When are you going to _____?
   a. put away them
   b. hang up them
   c. hear from them
   d. drop off them

3. Think _____.
   a. it over
   b. it around
   c. it about
   d. over it

4. Don't _____.
   a. pick your brother on
   b. pick him on
   c. pick on him
   d. pick up him

5. Did you _____?
   a. hand in it
   b. look for it
   c. do over it
   d. figure out it

6. Rita takes _____.
   a. out it
   b. off it
   c. me after
   d. after her father

G "CAN-DO" REVIEW

Match the "can do" statement and the correct sentence.

_____ **1.** I can give information about myself.

_____ **2.** I can give advice.

_____ **3.** I can express inability.

_____ **4.** I can express obligation.

_____ **5.** I can tell about future plans.

_____ **6.** I can describe things that haven't occurred yet.

_____ **7.** I can compare myself with another person.

_____ **8.** I can describe a person's background.

_____ **9.** I can describe a person's personality.

_____ **10.** I can invite someone to do something.

   a. I'd like to, but I can't.

   b. I've never done that.

   c. He's a very quiet person.

   d. I'm going to wash my car tomorrow.

   e. Would you like to see a movie with me today?

   f. I'm a vegetarian.

   g. My mother was born in a small town in Portugal.

   h. I think you should do it over.

   i. My brother and I are very different.

   j. I have to clean up my apartment.

A PERSONAL INFORMATION

STUDENT BOOK
PAGES **10a–10d**

Match the questions and answers.

_____ **1.** What's your phone number?

_____ **2.** What's your place of birth?

_____ **3.** What's your marital status?

_____ **4.** What's your height?

_____ **5.** What's your weight?

_____ **6.** What's your social security number?

_____ **7.** What's your date of birth?

a. I'm single.

b. I'm 145 pounds.

c. (212) 555–2283.

d. I'm 5 feet, 4 inches.

e. 2/23/90.

f. Santiago, Chile.

g. 012–65–3367.

B A PERSONAL INFORMATION FORM

Complete the form. Use any information you wish.

PERSONAL INFORMATION

Name _____
                          FIRST   MIDDLE   LAST

Address _____
             NUMBER   STREET   APT. #

_____ _____ _____   **E-Mail** _____
                          CITY   STATE   ZIP CODE

Home Phone _____   **Cell Phone**_____

SSN _____ – _____ – _____   **Date of Birth** _____   **Place of Birth** _____

Height _____ feet _____ inches **Weight** _____ pounds

Hair Color _____   **Eye Color** _____

Marital Status (CIRCLE ONE):   single   married   divorced   widowed

FAMILY MEMBERS IN HOUSEHOLD

Name	Relationship	Name	Relationship
_____	_____	_____	_____
_____	_____	_____	_____
_____	_____	_____	_____
_____	_____	_____	_____
_____	_____	_____	_____

C PREVENTING IDENTITY THEFT

Read the article on student book page 10b. Decide if each statement is a good way to prevent identify theft. Write Y (Yes) or N (No).

_____ 1. Always carry your social security card.

_____ 2. Check your bank account statement once a year.

_____ 3. Don't throw credit card receipts in the trash.

_____ 4. Shred your paychecks.

_____ 5. Call your credit card company if a statement doesn't arrive when it should.

_____ 6. Don't go away from home for several days.

D THREE BRANCHES OF GOVERNMENT

Use these words to complete the civics lesson.

appoint	declare	law	Senate
armed forces	enforces	legislative	Senators
Cabinet	executive	makes	signs
Commander	interprets	President	Supreme Court
Congress	judicial	representatives	Vice President

The _____ ^{1} branch of government has two parts—the House

of Representatives and the _____ ^{2}. This branch of government is

also called _____ ^{3}. It _____ ^{4} the laws. It can

also _____ ^{5} war. _____ ^{6} serve a six-year term,

and _____ ^{7} serve a two-year term.

The _____ ^{8} branch of government _____ ^{9}

the laws. The _____ ^{10} is chief executive of this branch and the

_____ ^{11}-in-Chief of the _____ ^{12}. Members of

the _____ ^{13} give advice to the President. When the President

_____ ^{14} bills that Congress writes, they become _____ ^{15}.

The President can serve two four-year terms. If the President dies before the end of the

term, the _____ ^{16} becomes the new President.

The _____ ^{17} branch of government _____ ^{18} the laws.

There are nine justices in the _____ ^{19}. They serve a life term. When they

retire or die, the President can _____ ^{20} a new justice.

A APOLOGIZING FOR LATENESS AT WORK

Match the correct sentence parts.

_____ 1. I had a flat   **a.** terrible.

_____ 2. I had an   **b.** doctor.

_____ 3. I had to go to the   **c.** accident.

_____ 4. I missed the   **d.** late.

_____ 5. Traffic was   **e.** tire.

_____ 6. The trains were running   **f.** bus.

B A TRAFFIC ACCIDENT REPORT FORM

Imagine you were in a car accident. Complete the traffic accident report.

REPORT OF TRAFFIC ACCIDENT

9 - DIAGRAM

WEATHER CONDITIONS

01 Clear
02 Cloudy
03 Fog
04 Rain
05 Snow

ROAD SURFACE

01 Dry
02 Wet
03 Slippery
04 Icy

LIGHT CONDITIONS

01 Dawn
02 Daylight
03 Dusk
04 Dark

DESCRIBE WHAT HAPPENED:

C U.S. HISTORY 1

Complete the history facts.

> Constitution   England   Philadelphia
> Declaration of Independence   John Hancock   Thomas Jefferson

1. The Revolutionary War was between _____ and its American colonies.
2. _____ wrote the Declaration of Independence.
3. The most famous signature on the U.S. Constitution belongs to _____.
4. The U.S. _____ describes the powers of the national and state governments.
5. _____ was an important meeting place in early U.S. history.
6. The _____ says that all people have certain rights.

D U.S. HISTORY 2

Complete the paragraphs.

> Civil War   Constitution   North   Revolutionary War
> Colonial   father   President   South

George Washington was the leader of the _____ [1] Army. After the

_____ [2] ended, Washington worked with other leaders to write the

_____ [3]. Then he became the first _____ [4] of the

United States. People say he is the "_____"[5] of the nation.

The _____ [6] was an American war between the Northern and

Southern states. The _____ [7] had cotton farms with slaves. The

_____ [8] was against slavery. The North and the South fought against

each other from 1861 to 1865.

E U.S. HISTORY 3: *TIMELINE*

Match the years and the events in U.S. history.

_____ 1. 1789   **a.** Abraham Lincoln signed the Emancipation Proclamation.

_____ 2. 1861   **b.** Martin Luther King, Jr. led the March on Washington.

_____ 3. 1863   **c.** The Civil War ended.

_____ 4. 1865   **d.** The Civil War began.

_____ 5. 1963   **e.** The Immigration Act gave everyone the right to apply to come to the U.S.

_____ 6. 1965   **f.** George Washington became the first President of the United States.

A CALLING IN SICK AT WORK

Put the conversation in the correct order. Number the lines 1–7.

_____ If I feel better tomorrow, I'll come to work.

_____ I'm calling to say I won't be able to work today. I have a bad stomachache.

__1__ Hello. Acme Company.

_____ Okay. Thanks for calling.

_____ I'm sorry to hear that.

_____ Good morning, Ms. Brant.

_____ Hello. This is Amy Brant.

B CALLING SCHOOL TO REPORT A CHILD'S ABSENCE

Write the correct words to complete the conversation.

attendance	name	sore	tone
fever	reason	This	won't

A. This is the school _____ ¹ line. After the _____ ², please give your

_____ ³, your child's name, and the _____ ⁴ for your child's absence.

Thank you.

B. Hello. _____ ⁵ is Liu Chou. My son Chong _____ ⁶ be in school today.

He has a _____ ⁷ throat and a high _____ ⁸.

C A NOTE TO THE TEACHER

Write the correct words to complete the note.

absent	attendance	homework	September 29
appointment	Dear	school	Sincerely

_____ ¹

_____ ² Ms. Ramirez,

My son Roland will be _____ ³ from _____ ⁴ tomorrow. I have to take him

to a medical _____ ⁵. I will call the school's _____ ⁶ line in the morning. Please

send me a message to let me know the _____ ⁷ for the next day. Thank you very much.

_____ ⁸,

Wanda Vacano

Complete the sentences with information from the map.

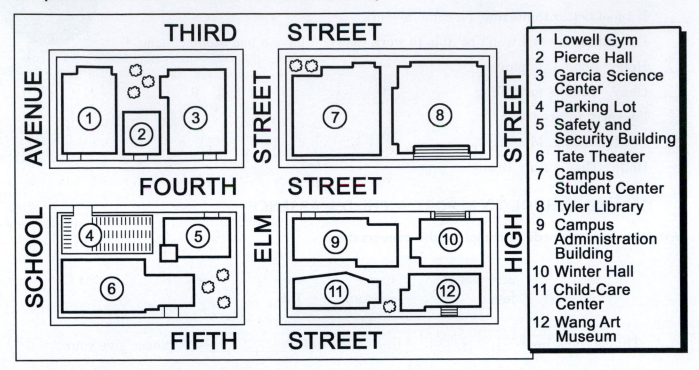

1. The _____ is on the corner of Fifth Street and School Avenue.

2. The Safety and Security Building is next to the _____.

3. Pierce Hall is between Lowell Gym and the _____.

4. The Wang Art Museum is on _____ Street.

5. Winter Hall is across from the _____.

6. If you need a parking permit, go to Building number _____.

7. If you need a copy of your grades, go to Building number _____.

8. You can swim and play basketball in Building number _____.

9. You can learn about student clubs and activities in Building number _____.

10. Science classes are on the corner of Fourth Street and _____.

A EMPLOYMENT APPLICATION VOCABULARY

Match the employment application section and the correct information.

_____	1. Position you are applying for	a.	Safeguard Insurance Company
_____	2. Education history	b.	583 Pond Avenue, Millersville, PA
_____	3. Personal information – Address	c.	Ms. Juanita Tompkins
_____	4. Skills	d.	January 2016 – present
_____	5. Current place of employment	e.	Office assistant
_____	6. Dates of employment	f.	Filing, typing, Spanish
_____	7. Reference	g.	Lincoln High School, Glenwood College

4 STUDENT BOOK PAGES **50a–50d**

B APPLYING FOR A JOB

Complete the conversations with the correct words.

application	current	former	references
apply for	dates of employment	position	skills
complete	education history		

1. A. What kind of _____ are you looking for?

   B. I would like to work in an office. I have many office _____. I can use a computer, I can type, and I can take messages.

2. A. I would like to _____ the office assistant job.

   B. Okay. Here's an _____ form. Please _____ it and bring it back it me.

3. A. Do I need to list _____?

   B. Yes. Please write the names and phone numbers of three people we can talk to in order to learn more about you.

4. A. What is your _____ job?

   B. Right now I'm working as a receptionist at Bell Systems.

5. A. Tell me about your _____ jobs.

   B. For one year I worked as a salesperson. Before that I worked as a cashier.

6. A. What is your _____?

   B. I graduated from high school in 2016. Then I went to Lewiston Community College for two years.

7. A. What are your _____ at Kippy's Hardware?

   B. I worked there from 2014 to 2017.

A JOB APPLICATION FORM

Complete the form. Use any information you wish.

NAME _____	DATE _____
Last First Middle	SOCIAL SECURITY NUMBER _____
ADDRESS _____	TELEPHONE NUMBER _____

EMPLOYMENT HISTORY (LIST MOST RECENT OR PRESENT EXPERIENCE FIRST)

Date	Name & Address of Employer	Position	Salary	Name of Supervisor	Reason for Leaving
From: To:					
Duties					
From: To:					
Duties					
From: To:					
Duties					
From: To:					
Duties					
From: To:					
Duties					
From: To:					
Duties					

EDUCATION HISTORY

High School _____

    NAME   CITY   STATE

Diploma or GED Received: Yes _____   No _____   Date _____

College/Continuing Education   Location   Field of Study   Degree/Certification

SKILLS

List any special training or skills you have.

REFERENCES (No relatives please)

    Name   Relationship   Telephone Number

1. _____

2. _____

A DESCRIBING EMPLOYMENT HISTORY

Write the correct words to complete the conversation.

before	for	job	means	since	understand
did	incarcerated	long	now	terminated	

A. Where do you work _____1?

B. I work at Home Hardware.

A. How _____2 have you worked there?

B. I've worked there _____3 September, 2016.

A. Where did you work _____4 that?

B. I worked at Joseph's Construction.

A. How long _____5 you work there?

B. I worked there _____6 two years.

A. Have you ever been _____7?

B. I'm sorry. I don't understand what that _____8.

A. Have you ever been fired from a _____9?

B. I _____10. No, I haven't.

A. Have you ever been _____11?

B. No, I haven't.

B A COVER LETTER AND RESUME

Read the cover letter and resume on student book page 64b. Decide if each statement is True (T) or False (F).

_____ **1.** Monica Jordan is applying for a job.

_____ **2.** Linda Palermo works as a restaurant manager.

_____ **3.** Linda worked as a waitress at the Ocean House in Miami.

_____ **4.** Monica's office is in Sunrise, Florida.

_____ **5.** Linda had two different jobs at the Health Food Markets in Miami.

_____ **6.** A friend told Linda about the job at the Seaside Restaurant.

_____ **7.** Linda supervises 15 employees in her current job.

_____ **8.** Linda put her telephone number in her cover letter.

WRITING A RESUME

Write your own resume. (Use any information you wish.)

_____
(Name)

_____
(Address)

_____
(Phone Number or E-mail)

WORK EXPERIENCE (LIST MOST RECENT FIRST)

Dates
FROM: _____   _____
                  (Position, Place of Employment)
TO: _____
                  _____
                  (City, State)

                  _____
                  (Description of job duties)

Dates
FROM: _____   _____
                  (Position, Place of Employment)
TO: _____
                  _____
                  (City, State)

                  _____
                  (Description of job duties)

Dates
FROM: _____   _____
                  (Position, Place of Employment)
TO: _____
                  _____
                  (City, State)

                  _____
                  (Description of job duties)

EDUCATION HISTORY

Dates
FROM: _____   _____
                  (Degree or certification)
TO: _____
                  _____
                  (School, City, State)

Dates
FROM: _____   _____
                  (Degree or certification)
TO: _____
                  _____
                  (School, City, State)

SKILLS

(List special skills here, for example: languages you speak, typing or computer skills, machine operating skills, any special license you have to drive or operate equipment, etc.)

_____

_____

_____

_____

_____

Write a cover letter to apply for a job.

_____

_____
(your address)

_____
(today's date)

_____

_____

_____

Dear _____,

I would like to apply for the position of _____.

I saw your advertisement _____. As you can see

from my resume, I have the experience and skills to _____.

I have worked in _____ for _____.
(period of time)

I look forward to hearing from you to arrange an interview.

Sincerely,

_____
(your signature)

_____
(your name printed)

E AN EMPLOYEE MANUAL

Read the employee manual on student book page 64c. Decide if each statement is True (T) or False (F).

_____ 1. Full-time employees get three fifteen-minute breaks a day.

_____ 2. Full-time employees work Monday through Sunday.

_____ 3. Employees punch in at the end of the day.

_____ 4. Supervisors must sign the employee timesheet or time card.

_____ 5. Employees are allowed to punch in for each other.

_____ 6. Employees can pick up their checks at 4:00 P.M. on Friday afternoon.

_____ 7. Direct deposit sends your paycheck directly to your home.

_____ 8. Employees get two weeks of sick leave every year.

_____ 9. Employees can save up their sick days and use them in the future.

_____ 10. Employees can save up their vacation days and use them in the future.

A   LEASE VOCABULARY

Match the words that have the same meaning.

_____ 1. permitted   a. garbage
_____ 2. lease   b. apartment
_____ 3. prohibited   c. not allowed
_____ 4. trash   d. rental agreement
_____ 5. leased premises   e. dogs, cats, animals
_____ 6. pets   f. allowed

B   PAYING BILLS

Pay the utility bills on student book pages 80b and 80c. Complete the money order and the two checks.

MONEY ORDER			
Serial Number	Month–Day–Year	Post Office	U.S. Dollars and Cents
02978251423	11-09-20	90020	$89.91

Amount: EIGHTY-NINE & 91 ###############

PAY TO: _____

ADDRESS: _____

NEGOTIABLE ONLY IN THE U.S.

FROM: _____

ADDRESS: _____

CLERK: 017

⑈00030453 2⑆ 02978251423

1121

DATE _____

PAY TO THE
ORDER OF _____ $ [_____]

_____ Dollars

WELLINGTON SAVINGS BANK

Memo _____   _____

⑈798599331⑆ 88823922 1121

1122

DATE _____

PAY TO THE
ORDER OF _____ $ [_____]

_____ Dollars

WELLINGTON SAVINGS BANK

Memo _____   _____

⑈798599331⑆ 88823922 1122

BANK FORMS

Complete the withdrawal slip. Withdraw $50.00. Your account number is 402749635.

NATIONAL FIRST BANK   **WITHDRAWAL**

Date

                                                    ACCOUNT NUMBER

Name (Print)

Signature _____   Total $

⑆311098 79⑈

Complete the deposit slip. Deposit one check for $125.00, one check for $25.00, and $40.00 in cash.

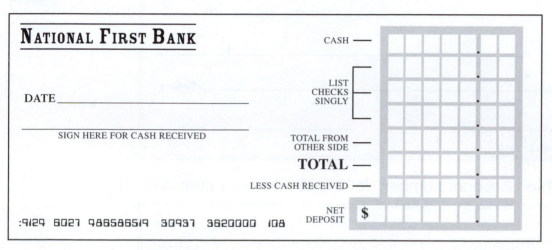

NATIONAL FIRST BANK   CASH ——

                                      LIST
DATE_____   CHECKS
                                      SINGLY

   SIGN HERE FOR CASH RECEIVED
                                      TOTAL FROM ——
                                      OTHER SIDE
                                      TOTAL ——
                                      LESS CASH RECEIVED ——

                                      NET $
⑆9129 8027 988588519 30937 3820000 108   DEPOSIT

Complete the deposit slip. Deposit one check for $200.00 and one check for $140.00, and receive $100.00 in cash.

NATIONAL FIRST BANK   CASH ——

                                      LIST
DATE_____   CHECKS
                                      SINGLY

   SIGN HERE FOR CASH RECEIVED
                                      TOTAL FROM ——
                                      OTHER SIDE
                                      TOTAL ——
                                      LESS CASH RECEIVED ——

                                      NET $
⑆9129 8027 988588519 30937 3820000 108   DEPOSIT

BALANCING A CHECKBOOK

Write the following checks.

To: Northwest Power   Account number: 210 2423   Amount due: $43.15

	151
	DATE _____ 20 _____
PAY TO THE ORDER OF _____	$ [_____]
_____ Dollars	
Memo _____	_____
:233157221O: 2 2915387 151	

To: Com-Phone   Account number: 1223134   Amount due: $51.20

	152
	DATE _____ 20 _____
PAY TO THE ORDER OF _____	$ [_____]
_____ Dollars	
Memo _____	_____
:233157221O: 2 2915387 152	

To: Viewcast Cable   Account number: 76089335   Amount due: $78.90

	153
	DATE _____ 20 _____
PAY TO THE ORDER OF _____	$ [_____]
_____ Dollars	
Memo _____	_____
:233157221O: 2 2915387 153	

Now write the check information in the checkbook register and balance the checkbook.

Number	Date	Transaction	Debit	Credit	Balance
150	4/5/20	Water Company	41.50		899.50

E A RENTAL APARTMENT ACCEPTANCE FORM

What problems does this apartment have? Complete the form.

	Apartment Acceptance Form		
Name _____		Date _____	
Address _____		Apt. # _____	

	NOTE PROBLEMS BELOW	Acceptable?	
		Yes	No
Walls & Ceilings			
Floors			
Electrical Fixtures			
Plumbing Fixtures			
Other			

This form must be returned to the rental office within five days of moving into the apartment.

_____   _____
APARTMENT MANAGER   TENANT

F READING THE YELLOW PAGES

Read the yellow pages and write the telephone number you should call.

HARDWARE

Contractor's Discount Hardware
21 Baker Carl .... (254) 889–1327

Economy Hardware – see our ad this page
24 High Clif .... (254) 298–9911

HARDWOOD

Southern Hardwood Supply
52 Essex Clif .... (254) 536–9121

Top Floor Hardwoods – see our ad this page
201 Elm Carl .... (254) 889–7745

HEATING CONTRACTORS

Ajax Air Conditioning & Heating
167 Washington Carl .... (254) 889–6162

Holmes Heating Corp – see our ad this page
52 Lakeview Burl .... (254) 536–2113

Economy Hardware

All bathroom and kitchen plumbing fixtures

Open 5:00 AM – 6:00 PM every day
24 High Street, Clifton (254) 298–9911

Top Floor Hardwoods

Supply
Installation
Repair

201 Elm Avenue, Carlton (254) 889–7745

HOLMES HEATING CORP
HEATING & PLUMBING
24 HOUR EMERGENCY SERVICE
52 LAKEVIEW ROAD, BURLINGTON
(254) 536–2113

1. You're looking for a new kitchen sink and bathtub.

   _____

2. Your air conditioning just broke.

   _____

3. You are a contractor in Clifton. You need some building materials.

   _____

4. It's 10:00 at night. A pipe broke and is leaking all over the floor.

   _____

5. You need someone to fix your wood floor.

   _____

A · REQUESTS AT WORK

Write the correct words to complete the conversations.

borrow	hang	lend	please	Thanks
copying	happy	lending	tables	welcome

STUDENT BOOK
PAGES 94a–94d

1. A. Would you please _____ me your dictionary?

   B. Sure. I'll be _____ to.

2. A. Thank you for _____ me your pen.

   B. You're _____.

3. A. Would you _____ set up the _____ for the meeting?

   B. Sure.

4. A. Could I possibly _____ a pencil?

   B. Sure.

   A. _____.

5. A. Thank you for _____ the report.

   B. No problem.

6. A. Would you please _____ the dresses on the racks?

   B. Sure.

B · WORKPLACE NOTES

Notes usually follow an order. Number the notes below according to these guidelines.
Write _1_, _2_, or _3_ before each line.

A Written Request	A Thank-You Note
1. Make the request.	1. Express appreciation for the person's help.
2. Explain why you need the help.	2. Explain how the person's help made a difference.
3. Repeat the request.	3. Express appreciation again.

Memorandum	Memo

Marco,
 	
____ Would you please choose the best ones and pass them to me?
 	
____ I need some pictures for the PowerPoint presentation. I think you might have some on file.
 	
_1_ Would you be able to help me with my presentation?
     Thanks,
     Sam
	Marco,
	
	____ Your pictures made the presentation so much more interesting.
	
	____ Thanks again for your assistance.
	
	____ Thank you for helping out with the presentation the other day.
	     Sam

Now write a note to a classmate or to your teacher. Make a request.

Maria completed this W-4 form at work. The form gives her employer information about how much money to withhold from her paycheck for federal taxes. Read the form and answer the questions below.

Personal Allowances Worksheet

A   Enter "1" for **yourself** if no one else can claim you as a dependent. - **A** __1__

B   Enter "1" if   {   • You are single and have only one job; or
                 • You are married, have only one job and your spouse does not work; or
                 • Your wages from a second job or your spouse's wages (or the total of both) are $1,500 or less. } - - - **B** _____

C   Enter "1" for your **spouse**. - **C** __1__

D   Enter the number of **dependents** (other than your spouse or yourself). - **D** __1__

E   Enter "1" if you will file as **head of household** on your tax return. - **E** _____

F   Enter "1" if you have at least $2,000 of **child or dependent care expenses**. - - - - - - - - - - - - - - - - - **F** __1__

G   **Child Tax Credit**
      • If your total income will be less than $70,000 ($100,000 if married), enter "2" for each child.
      • If your total income will be between $70,000 and $84,000 ($100,000 and $119,000 if
        married), enter "1" for each child. - **G** __1__

H   Add lines A through G and enter total amount here. - ▶ **H** __5__

Stop here and enter the number from line H on line 5 of Form W-4 below.

Form **W-4**   **Employee's Withholding Allowance Certificate**

1 Type or print your first name and middle initial.	Last name	**2** Your social security number
Maria A.	Montero	222 : 111 : 5555

Home address (number and street or rural route)	**3** ☐ Single ☒ Married ☐ Married, but withhold at higher Single rate.
2102 Western Drive	

City or town, state, and ZIP code	**4** If your last name is different from the one on your social security card, check here. You must call 1-800-772-1213 for a replacement card. ☐
San Antonio, Texas 78201	

5 Total number of allowances you are claiming (from line **H** above) - - - - - - - - - -	**5**	5
6 Additional amount, if any, you want withheld from each paycheck - - - - - - - - - -	**6**	

7 I claim exemption from withholding for 2020, and I meet **both** of the following conditions.
   • Last year I had a right to a refund of **all** federal income tax withheld because I had **no** tax liability **and**
   • This year I expect a refund of **all** federal income tax withheld because I expect to have **no** tax liability.
   If you meet both conditions write "Exempt" here -   **7**

8 Under penalties of perjury, I declare that I have examined this certificate and to the best of my knowledge and belief, it is true, correct, and complete.

Employee's signature	**Date**
Maria A. Montero	10/06/20

---

1.   Is Maria married? _____

2.   Is Maria the head of the household? _____

3.   How many children do Maria and her husband have? _____

4.   What is Maria and her husband's total income?

     Between _____ and _____.

D READING A PAYCHECK AND PAY STUB

Read the paycheck and pay stub and answer the questions.

Teknon, Inc.				Angela Suarez. Employee No. 2331
				Pay Period 04/29/19 – 05/12/19

Earnings	Rate	Hours	This Period	Year to Date
Regular	12.00	40	480.00	4,320.00
Overtime	18.00	5	90.00	810.00
Gross Pay			**570.00**	5,130.00

Taxes & Deductions				
Federal Tax	—	—	59.00	531.00
State Tax	—	—	28.00	252.00
FICA/Medicare	—	—	42.00	378.00
Total			129.00	1,161.00
Net Pay			**441.00**	3,969.00

	6513
Teknon, Incorporated	DATE _____5/15/19_____
PAY TO Angela Suarez	$	$441.00

Four hundred forty-one and 00/100 _____ Dollars

Nien Tran

:788795261 : 36455670" 6513

1. What is Angela's regular rate of pay? _____

2. How many regular hours did Angela work this pay period? _____

3. How many overtime hours did she work this pay period? _____

4. How much money did Angela earn before taxes and deductions this pay period? _____

5. How much money did Angela's employer take out in taxes and deductions this pay period? _____

6. How much is Angela's paycheck for this pay period? _____

7. How much has Angela earned this year before taxes and deductions? _____

8. How much money has Angela's employer taken out in taxes and deductions this year? _____

9. How much has Angela taken home in earnings after all taxes and deductions this year? _____

A SCHEDULING MEDICAL APPOINTMENTS

Write the correct words to complete the conversations.

make	cancel	confirm	reschedule

STUDENT BOOK
PAGES **110a–110f**

1. A. Hello. This is Yasmin Ibrahim. I'd like to _____ an appointment.

   B. Can you come in on Monday, January 25th at 11:30?

   A. Yes. Thank you.

2. A. Hello. This is Yasmin Ibrahim. I'm calling to _____ my appointment on Monday, January 25th at 11:30.

   B. Yes. You have an appointment at 11:30 on Monday, January 25th. See you then.

3. A. Hello. This is Yasmin Ibrahim. I need to _____ my appointment on Monday, January 25th at 11:30.

   B. Okay. Would you like to _____ that appointment?

   A. No. Not at this time. Thanks very much.

B INTERNAL ORGANS

Write these words on the correct lines.

colon	heart	kidneys	lungs
gall bladder	intestine	liver	stomach

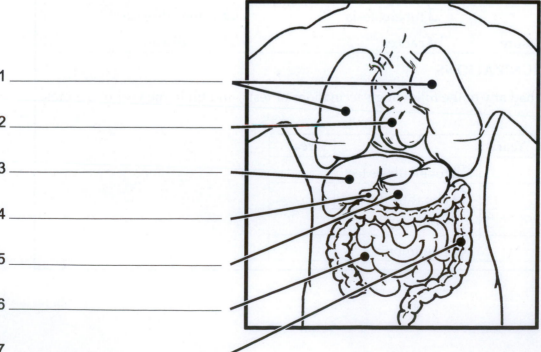

1 _____

2 _____

3 _____

4 _____

5 _____

6 _____

7 _____

MEDICAL HISTORY

Name _____ Date of Birth __ __ / __ __ / __ __ __ __

List the medications you are now taking. Include non-prescription drugs and vitamins.

_____

List any allergies you have to drugs, food, or other items.

_____

List any operations you have had, including the year.

_____

Please check if you have had any of the following health problems.

❏ chicken pox	❏ diabetes	❏ depression
❏ measles	❏ tuberculosis	❏ frequent earaches
❏ mumps	❏ cancer	❏ severe headaches
❏ asthma	❏ AIDS	❏ back problems
❏ heart disease	❏ kidney disease	❏ frequent colds
❏ high blood pressure	❏ liver disease (hepatitis)	❏ stomach problems
❏ pneumonia	❏ influenza	❏ loss of appetite

FAMILY HISTORY

Please check if anyone in your family (parents, siblings, grandparents, children) has had any of the following illnesses.

❏ asthma	❏ diabetes	❏ AIDS
❏ heart disease	❏ tuberculosis	❏ kidney disease
❏ high blood pressure	❏ cancer	❏ liver disease

RECORD OF IMMUNIZATIONS

Please check if you had any of the following vaccinations or tests, and fill in the year of the most recent ones.

	Year		Year
❏ measles		❏ tuberculosis test	
❏ mumps		❏ hepatitis B	
❏ chicken pox		❏ influenza	
❏ tetanus		❏ pneumonia	

IMMUNIZATIONS

Read the immunization schedule on student book page 110d. Put check marks to complete this vaccination chart.

	at birth	2 months	4 months	6 months	12 months	15 months	18 months	2–3 years	4–6 years
Hepatitis B	✔		✔			✔			
Diphtheria,Tetanus, Pertussis (DTaP)									
Polio									
Measles, Mumps, Rubella (MMR)									
Varicella (Chicken Pox)									

E **RECIPES AND NUTRITION**

Read the article *Healthy Eating and a Balanced Diet* on student book page 110e and answer the nutrition questions about this recipe.

Chicken Stew
(For 8 servings)

Ingredients:
8 pieces of chicken
1/2 cup of skim milk
1 cup of water
1 medium onion
1 1/2 teaspoons salt
1/2 teaspoon black pepper
3 tomatoes, chopped
1/4 cup celery, chopped
1 1/2 cups medium potatoes, peeled and chopped
1/2 cup carrots, chopped

1. Cut the extra fat and skin from the chicken.
2. Combine skim milk, water, chicken, onion, salt, pepper, and tomatoes. Cover and cook over low heat for 25 minutes.
3. Add celery, potatoes, carrots and continue to cook for 15 more minutes.

Each serving provides:
206 calories
6 grams of fat
75 milligrams of cholesterol
2 grams of fiber
28 grams of protein

1. Which four ingredients include fiber? _____

2. Which ingredient provides protein? _____

3. Which ingredient provides cholesterol? _____

F **RECIPE MEASUREMENTS**

Use the recipe measurement table. Double the Chicken Stew recipe in Exercise E.

3 teaspoons = 1 tablespoon	16 tablespoons = 1 cup	2 cups = 1pint

For 16 servings:

1 _____ of skim milk   _____ tomatoes, chopped

1 _____ of water   _____ cup celery, chopped

_____ medium onions   _____ cups medium potatoes, peeled and chopped

1 _____ salt   _____ cup carrots, chopped

_____ teaspoon black pepper

A RETURNING A DEFECTIVE PRODUCT

Write the correct words to complete the conversation.

exchange	missing	refund	stained
matter	receipt	return	

A. I'd like to _____ ¹ this shirt.

B. What's the _____ ² with it?

A. Two buttons are _____ ³ and the sleeve is _____ ⁴.

B. Would you like to _____ ⁵ it? We can find another one that isn't defective.

A. No, thank you. I'd like a _____ ⁶, please. Here's my _____ ⁷.

B SALE PRICES

Read the advertisement and answer the questions.

JAMIESON'S DEPARTMENT STORE
Once-a-Year Sale

Men's Suits
40% off
NOW $96–$168
Were $160–$280

60% Savings on Women's Dresses
Orig. $90–$160
Reduced to $36–$64

Men's Clancy Sports Jackets
Buy one, get one half price
Reg. $80–$150

Women's Blouses
2 for $45 or 3 for $60
(original $29.99–$36.99)

Women's Skirts
Half Price!
Reg. $50–$70
Sale $25–$35

Men's Dress Shirts
2 for $55 or $29.99 each

1. The sale price for a $200 men's suit is _____.

2. If you buy two Clancy men's sports jackets with an original price of $90 each, you pay _____.

3. With the sale price, you save _____ on a $90 women's dress.

4. If you buy one men's dress shirt, you pay _____.

(continued)

5. If you buy four men's dress shirts, you pay _____ .

6. When you buy a women's skirt with a regular price of $60, the sale price is _____ .

7. When you buy three women's blouses, you pay _____ for each one.

8. If you buy a men's suit on sale for $168, you save _____ .

C SUPERMARKET COUPON MATH

Read the coupons and answer the questions.

1. One loaf of Lindy's Whole Wheat Bread costs $3.49. How much do you pay with the coupon? _____

2. You can use the coupon for Lindy's Whole Wheat Bread until what date? _____

3. Each can of Mama Lisa's soup costs $2.75. If you buy two cans with the coupon, how much do you pay for each can? _____

4. Each box of Italo's Pasta costs $1.75. If you buy three boxes with the coupon, how much do you pay? _____

5. Can you use the Sunny's Orange Juice coupon on a half-gallon of juice? _____

6. Each bag of Classic Chips is $3.25. How much are three bags with the coupon? _____

7. Each can of Del Montana Organic Tomatoes is $1.50. If you buy three cans with the coupon, how much is each can? _____

A JOB PERFORMANCE EVALUATION

How well do you do your job? Evaluate your own performance at work.
Complete the form.

JOB PERFORMANCE EVALUATION FORM

Name: _____

Evaluation Date: _____ Position: _____

Knowledge of Job Does the employee understand the job well? Does the employee have all the skills necessary for the job? Does the employee keep up with training opportunities to learn new skills for the job?	Excellent ☐ Good ☐ Needs Improvement ☐ Unsatisfactory ☐
Communication Does the employee communicate clearly? Does the employee listen to co-workers and supervisors? Does the employee learn from feedback?	Excellent ☐ Good ☐ Needs Improvement ☐ Unsatisfactory ☐
Teamwork Does the employee get along with co-workers? Is the employee polite and friendly with co-workers? Is the employee helpful to others? Does the employee have a positive attitude?	Excellent ☐ Good ☐ Needs Improvement ☐ Unsatisfactory ☐
Problem Solving Does the employee make efficient decisions? Does the employee solve problems creatively?	Excellent ☐ Good ☐ Needs Improvement ☐ Unsatisfactory ☐
Customer Relations Is the employee polite and friendly with customers?	Excellent ☐ Good ☐ Needs Improvement ☐ Unsatisfactory ☐
Personal Appearance Does the employee dress appropriately? Is the employee well groomed?	Excellent ☐ Good ☐ Needs Improvement ☐ Unsatisfactory ☐
Dependability Does the employee come to work on time? Is the employee dependable and hardworking? Does the employee finish work on time?	Excellent ☐ Good ☐ Needs Improvement ☐ Unsatisfactory ☐

Employee's Signature _____ Date _____
(Signature means that the employee was given the opportunity to discuss the evaluation with the
supervisor)

Evaluated by _____ Date _____

CONTINUING EDUCATION OPPORTUNITIES

Read the information about ways to continue your education and answer the questions.

Adult education centers offer introductory classes in many fields. They do not provide certification or a degree.

Vocational/Technical schools teach students specific skills such as auto mechanics or heating and air-conditioning repair. These schools provide training and certification to prepare their students for employment in a technical field.

Community colleges provide a two-year Associate's degree. They prepare students for jobs such as nurse assistants, child-care providers, or office managers. They also prepare students to continue their education at a four-year college.

Four-year colleges provide a Bachelor's degree. They prepare students for jobs such as nurses, teachers, or computer programmers. Some students finish four-year colleges and then continue in a **graduate school** to learn a profession, such as medicine or law.

Online courses are classes on the Internet. Adult education centers, community colleges, and four-year colleges offer online courses. Some of these classes are free. Other classes are part of a certification or degree program and have a fee.

1. What kinds of schools have you attended? _____

_____

_____

2. What kind of school would you like to attend in the future? _____

_____

_____

C **YOUR EDUCATION PLAN**

What skills do you want to learn? Where can you learn them? When do you plan to continue your education? Complete your education plan in detail.

My Education Plan
What I plan to study:
Where:
When:

Listening Scripts

Page 7 Exercise H

Listen to each question and then complete the answer.

1. Does Jim like to play soccer?
2. Is Alice working today?
3. Are those students staying after school today?
4. Do Mr. and Mrs. Jackson work hard?
5. Does your wife still write poetry?
6. Is it raining?
7. Is he busy?
8. Do you have to leave?
9. Does your sister play the violin?
10. Is your brother studying in the library?
11. Are you wearing a necklace today?
12. Do you and your husband go camping very often?
13. Is your niece doing her homework?
14. Are they still chatting online?
15. Do you and your friends play Scrabble very often?

Page 13 Exercise B

Listen and circle the correct answer.

1. They work.
2. They worked.
3. We study English.
4. I waited for the bus.
5. We visit our friends.
6. She met important people.
7. He taught Chinese.
8. She delivers the mail.
9. I wrote letters to my friends.
10. I ride my bicycle to work.
11. He sleeps very well.
12. I had a terrible headache.

Page 26 Exercise C

Listen and choose the time of the action.

1. My daughter is going to sing Broadway show tunes in her high school show.
2. Janet bought a new dress for her friend's party.
3. Are you going to go out with George?
4. I went shopping at the new mall.
5. How did you poke yourself in the eye?
6. Who's going to prepare dinner?
7. Did the baby sleep well?
8. I'm really looking forward to Saturday night.
9. Is your son going to play games on his computer?
10. We're going to complain to the landlord about the heat in our apartment.
11. We bought a dozen donuts.
12. I'm going to take astronomy.

Page 33 Exercise L

Listen to each story. Then answer the questions.

What Are Mr. and Mrs. Miller Looking Forward to?

Mr. and Mrs. Miller moved into their new house in Los Angeles last week. They're happy because the house has a large, bright living room and a big, beautiful yard. They're looking forward to life in their new home. Every weekend they'll be able to relax in their living room and enjoy the beautiful California weather in their big, beautiful yard. But this weekend Mr. and Mrs. Miller won't be relaxing. They're going to be very busy. First, they're going to repaint the living room. Then, they're going to assemble their new computer and VCR. And finally, they're going to plant some flowers in their yard. They'll finally be able to relax NEXT weekend.

What's Jonathan Looking Forward to?

I'm so excited! I'm sitting at my computer in my office, but I'm not thinking about my work today. I'm thinking about next weekend because next Saturday is the day I'll be getting married. After the wedding, my wife and I will be going to Hawaii for a week. I can't wait! For one week, we won't be working, we won't be cooking, we won't be cleaning, and we won't be paying bills. We'll be swimming in the ocean, relaxing on the beach, and eating in fantastic restaurants.

What's Mrs. Grant Looking Forward to?

Mrs. Grant is going to retire this year, and she's really looking forward to her new life. She won't be getting up early every morning and taking the bus to work. She'll be able to sleep late every day of the week. She'll read books, she'll work in her garden, and she'll go to museums with her friends. And she's very happy that she'll be able to spend more time with her grandchildren. She'll take them to the park to feed the birds, she'll take them to the zoo to see the animals, and she'll baby-sit when her son and daughter-in-law go out on Saturday nights.

Page 35 Exercise E

Listen to each question and then complete the answer.

Ex. Does your brother like to swim?
1. Are you going to buy donuts tomorrow?
2. Will Jennifer and John see each other again soon?
3. Doctor, did I sprain my ankle?
4. Does Tommy have a black eye?
5. Is your daughter practicing the violin?
6. Do you and your husband go to the movies very often?

7. Does Diane go out with her boyfriend every Saturday evening?

8. Will you and your wife be visiting us tonight?

Page 36 Exercise B

Listen and choose the word you hear.

1. I've ridden them for many years.
2. Yes. I've taken French.
3. I'm giving injections.
4. I've driven one for many years.
5. Yes. I've written it.
6. I'm drawing it right now.
7. I've spoken it for many years.
8. Yes. I've drawn that.

Page 37 Exercise D

Is Speaker B answering Yes or No? Listen to each conversation and circle the correct answer.

1. A. Do you know how to drive a bus?
   B. I've driven a bus for many years.

2. A. I usually take the train to work. Do you also take the train?
   B. Actually, I've never taken the train to work.

3. A. Are you a good swimmer?
   B. To tell the truth, I've never swum very well.

4. A. Did you get up early this morning?
   B. I've gotten up early every morning this week.

5. A. I'm going to give my dog a bath today. Do you have any advice?
   B. Sorry. I don't. I've never given my dog a bath.

6. A. Do you like to eat sushi?
   B. Of course! I've eaten sushi for many years.

7. A. I just got a big raise! Did you also get one?
   B. Actually, I've never gotten a raise.

8. A. I did very well on the math exam. How about you?
   B. I've never done well on a math exam.

Page 47 Exercise O

What things have these people done? What haven't they done? Listen and check Yes or No.

1. A. Carla, have you done your homework yet?
   B. Yes, I have. I did my homework this morning.
   A. And have you practiced the violin?
   B. No, I haven't practiced yet. I promise I'll practice this afternoon.

2. A. Kevin?
   B. Yes, Mrs. Blackwell?
   A. Have you written your report yet?
   B. No, I haven't. I'll write it immediately.
   A. And have you sent a fax to the Crane Company?
   B. No, I haven't. I promise I'll send them a fax after I write the report

3. A. Have you fed the dog yet?
   B. Yes, I have. I fed him a few minutes ago.
   A. Good. Well, I guess we can leave for work now.
   B. But we haven't eaten breakfast yet!

4. A. I'm leaving now, Mr. Green.
   B. Have you fixed the pipes in the basement, Charlie?
   A. Yes, I have.
   B. And have you repaired the washing machine?
   A. Yes, I have. It's working again.
   B. That's great! Thank you, Charlie.
   A. I'll send you a bill, Mr. Green.

5. A. You know, we haven't done the laundry all week.
   B. I know. We should do it today.
   A. We also haven't vacuumed the rugs!
   B. We haven't?
   A. No, we haven't.
   B. Oh. I guess we should vacuum them today.

6. A. Are we ready for the party?
   B. I think so. We've gotten all the food at the supermarket, and we've cleaned the house from top to bottom!
   A. Well, I guess we're ready for the party!

7. A. Have you spoken to the landlord about our broken light?
   B. Yes, I have. I spoke to him this morning.
   A. What did he say?
   B. He said we should call an electrician.
   A. Okay. Let's call Ajax Electric.
   B. Don't worry. I've already called them, and they're coming this afternoon.

8. A. Have you hooked up the new VCR yet?
   B. I can't do it. It's really difficult.
   A. Have you read the instructions?
   B. Yes, I have. I've read them ten times, and I still can't understand them!

Page 56 Exercise E

Listen and choose the correct answer.

1. Bob has been engaged since he got out of the army.
2. My sister Carol has been a professional musician since she finished music school.
3. Michael has been home since he fell and hurt himself last week.
4. My wife has gotten up early every morning since she started her new job.
5. Richard has eaten breakfast in the school cafeteria every morning since he started college.
6. Nancy and Tom have known each other for five and a half years.
7. My friend Charlie and I have played soccer every weekend since we were eight years old.

(continued)

8. Patty has had short hair since she was a teenager.
9. Ron has owned his own business since he moved to Chicago nine years ago.
10. I've been interested in astronomy for the past eleven years.
11. I use my personal computer all the time. I've had it since I was in high school.
12. Alan has had problems with his house since he bought it fifteen years ago.

Page 61 Exercise L

Listen and choose the correct answer.

1. A. Have you always been a salesperson?
   B. No. I've been a salesperson for the past four years. Before that, I was a cashier.

2. A. How long has your daughter been in medical school?
   B. She's been in medical school for the past two years.

3. A. Have your parents always lived in a house?
   B. No. They've lived in a house for the past ten years. Before that, they lived in an apartment.

4. A. How long have you wanted to be an actor?
   B. I've wanted to be an actor since I was in college. Before that, I wanted to be a musician.

5. A. Do you and your husband still exercise at your health club every day?
   B. No. We haven't done that for a year.

6. A. Has James been a bachelor all his life?
   B. No, he hasn't. He was married for ten years.

7. A. Has your sister Jane always wanted to be a writer?
   B. Yes, she has. She's wanted to be a writer all her life.

8. A. Have you ever broken your ankle?
   B. No. I've sprained it a few times, but I've never broken it.

9. A. Have you always liked classical music?
   B. No. I've liked classical music for the past few years. Before that, I liked rock music.

10. A. Has Billy had a sore throat for a long time?
    B. He's had a sore throat for the past two days. Before that, he had a fever.

11. A. Jennifer has been the store manager since last fall.
    B. What did she do before that?
    A. She was a salesperson.

12. A. Have you always been interested in modern art?
    B. No. I've been interested in modern art since I moved to Paris a few years ago. Before that, I was only interested in sports.

Page 64 Exercise E

Listen and choose the correct time expressions to complete the sentences.

1. A. How long have you been living there?
   B. I've been living there since . . .

2. A. How long has your daughter been practicing the piano?
   B. She's been practicing for . . .

3. A. How long have I been running?
   B. You've been running since . . .

4. A. How long have you been feeling bad?
   B. I've been feeling bad for . . .

5. A. How long have they been waiting?
   B. They've been waiting for . . .

6. A. How long has your son been studying?
   B. He's been studying since . . .

7. A. How long have your sister and her boyfriend been dating?
   B. They've been dating since . . .

8. A. Dad, how long have we been driving?
   B. Hmm. I think we've been driving for . . .

9. A. How long has your little girl been crying?
   B. She's been crying for . . .

Page 67 Exercise H

Listen and choose what the people are talking about.

1. She's been directing it for an hour.
2. We've been rearranging it all morning.
3. I've been paying them on time.
4. He's been playing them for years.
5. Have you been bathing them for a long time?
6. They've been rebuilding it for a year.
7. She's been writing it for a week.
8. He's been translating them for many years.
9. I've been reading it all afternoon.
10. She's been knitting them for a few weeks.
11. We've been listening to them all afternoon.
12. I've been recommending it for years.
13. They've been repairing it all day.
14. She's been taking it all morning.
15. I've been solving them all my life.

Page 71 Exercise L

Listen and decide where the conversation is taking place.

1. A. I'm really tired.
   B. No wonder! You've been chopping tomatoes for the past hour.

2. A. Mark! I'm surprised. You've been falling asleep in class all morning, and you've never fallen asleep in class before.
   B. I'm sorry, Mrs. Applebee. It won't happen again.

3. A. I've been washing these shirts for the past half hour, and they still aren't clean.
B. Here. Try this Presto Soap.

4. A. We've been standing in line for an hour and forty-five minutes.
B. I know. I hope the movie is good. I've never stood in line for such a long time.

5. A. What seems to be the problem, Mr. Jones?
B. My back has been hurting me for the past few days.
A. I'm sorry to hear that.

6. A. You know, we've been reading here for more than two hours.
B. You're right. I think it's time to go now.

7. A. Do you want to leave?
B. I think so. We've seen all the paintings here.

8. A. How long have you been exercising?
B. For an hour and a half.

9. A. We've been waiting for an hour, and it still isn't here.
B. I know. I'm going to be late for work.

10. A. I think we've seen them all. Which one do you want to buy?
B. I like that black one over there.

11. A. We've been watching this movie for the past hour, and it's terrible!
B. You're right. Let's change the channel.

12. A. I've got a terrible headache.
B. Why?
A. Customers have been complaining all morning.
B. What have they been complaining about?
A. Some people have been complaining about our terrible products, but most people have been complaining about our high prices.

Page 77 Exercise F

Listen and choose the correct answer.

1. A. How long has Janet been an actress?
B. She's been an actress since she graduated from acting school.

2. A. Have you watched the news yet?
B. Yes. I saw the president, and I heard his speech.

3. A. Have you always lived in Denver?
B. No. We've lived in Denver since 1995. Before that, we lived in New York.

4. A. Has Dad made dinner yet?
B. Not yet. He still has to make it.

5. A. How long has your ceiling been leaking?
B. It's been leaking for more than a week.
A. Have you called the superintendent?
B. Yes, I have. I've called him several times.

6. A. Billy is having trouble with his homework.
B. Has he asked anyone to help him?
A. No, he hasn't.

Page 87 Exercise N

Listen and choose the correct answer.

1. Dr. Gomez really enjoys . . .
2. Whenever possible, my wife and I try to avoid . . .
3. Next summer I'm going to learn . . .
4. Every day Rita practices . . .
5. My parents have decided . . .
6. I've considered . . .
7. Are you thinking about . . .
8. I'm going to quit . . .
9. Why do you keep on . . .
10. My doctor says I should stop . . .
11. David can't stand . . .
12. Are you going to continue to . . .
13. James doesn't want to start . . .
14. Next semester Kathy is going to begin . . .
15. You know, you can't keep on . . .

Page 97 Exercise J

Listen and choose the correct answer.

1. Steve lost his voice.
2. Is Beverly one of your relatives?
3. We just canceled our trip to South America.
4. Ricky has been failing all of his tests this year.
5. Francine dislocated her shoulder.
6. What did you and your students discuss in class?
7. My girlfriend and I rode on the roller coaster yesterday.
8. Grandma can't chew this piece of steak very well.
9. Jimmy loves my homemade food.
10. Did you see the motorcycles go by?
11. Do you think Mr. Montero will take a day off soon?
12. Amy wanted to ask her boss for a raise, but she got cold feet.
13. Have you heard that Margaret sprained her wrist?
14. I have to make an important decision.
15. I envy you.
16. I feel terrible. Debbie and Dan broke up last week.
17. My ankle hurts a lot.
18. I was heartbroken when I heard what happened.
19. Michael was furious with his neighbors.
20. We went to a recital last night.
21. Tom, don't forget to shine your shoes!
22. My friend Carla is extremely athletic.
23. My husband and I have been writing invitations all afternoon.
24. Charles rented a beautiful tuxedo for his niece's wedding.

Page 99 Exercise D

Listen and choose the correct answer.

Ex. My grandfather likes to . . .
1. Susan says she's going to stop . . .
2. My wife and I are thinking about . . .
3. David is considering . . .
4. I can't stand to . . .
5. You should definitely keep on . . .

Page 105 Exercise G

Listen and choose the correct answer.

1. A. I looked in the refrigerator, and I can't find the orange juice.
   B. That's because we . . .
2. A. I'm frustrated! My computer isn't working today.
   B. I think you forgot to . . .
3. A. What should I do with the Christmas decorations?
   B. I think it's time to . . .
4. A. Should I take these clothes to the cleaner's?
   B. Yes. You should definitely . . .
5. A. Hmm. What does this word mean?
   B. You should . . .
6. A. I have to return this skateboard to my cousin.
   B. When are you going to . . . ?
7. A. This math problem is very difficult.
   B. Maybe I can . . .
8. A. I'll never remember their new telephone number.
   B. You should . . .
9. A. I just spilled milk on the kitchen floor!
   B. Don't worry. I'll . . .

Page 108 Exercise L

Listen and choose the correct answer.

1. I really look up to my father.
2. My brother picks on me all the time.
3. Did you throw away the last can of paint?
4. I still haven't gotten over the flu.
5. Have you heard from your cousin Sam recently?
6. Why did you turn him down?
7. Did your French teacher call on you today?
8. George picked out a new suit for his wedding.
9. I have to drop my sister off at the airport.
10. Everything in the store is 20 percent off this week.
11. This jacket fits you.
12. Did you try on a lot of shoes?

Page 112 Exercise D

Listen and complete the sentences.

1. I missed the bus this morning.
2. I'm allergic to nuts.
3. I'll be on vacation next week.
4. I've never flown in a helicopter.
5. I can speak Chinese.
6. I like to go sailing.
7. I'm not going to the company picnic this weekend.
8. I saw a very good movie last night.
9. I don't go on many business trips.
10. I've been to London several times.
11. I'm not a vegetarian.
12. I should lose a little weight.
13. I can't stop worrying about my health.
14. I hate to drive downtown.
15. I won't be able to go to Nancy's party this Saturday night.

Page 117 Exercise K

Listen and complete the sentences.

1. I missed the bus today, . . .
2. I'm allergic to cats, . . .
3. I'll be on vacation next week, . . .
4. You've never seen a rainbow, . . .
5. I can speak Italian, . . .
6. I like to go sailing, . . .
7. I've been on television several times, . . .
8. I saw an exciting movie last weekend, . . .
9. I won't be in the office tomorrow, . . .
10. We were late, . . .
11. I'm not a vegetarian, . . .
12. I saw the stop sign, . . .
13. I can't swim very well, . . .
14. They have to work overtime this weekend, . . .
15. I won't be able to go to Sam's party this Friday night, . . .
16. I'm not afraid of flying, . . .
17. I haven't eaten breakfast yet, . . .
18. The other students weren't bored, . . .

Page 121 Exercise C

Listen and complete the sentences.

Ex. Nancy knows how to type, . . .
1. I'm interested in science, . . .
2. I won't be home this evening, . . .
3. I own my own business, . . .
4. I've never hooked up a computer, . . .
5. You just got a raise, . . .

UNIT 1

WORKBOOK PAGE 2

A. What's Happening?

1. What's, reading, She's reading
2. Where's, going, He's going
3. What's, watching, She's watching
4. What are, cooking, I'm cooking
5. Where are, moving, We're moving
6. Where are, sitting, They're sitting
7. What's, composing, He's composing
8. What are, baking, I'm baking

WORKBOOK PAGE 3

B. On the Phone

1. are
   I'm watching
   Is
   she is, She's taking
2. Are
   They're
   are they
   is doing
   is playing
   What are you
   I'm cooking
3. Is
   he isn't, He's exercising
   She's, She's fixing

WORKBOOK PAGE 4

C. You Decide: *Why Is Today Different?*

1. clean, I'm cleaning, . . .
2. irons, he's ironing, . . .
3. argue, we're arguing, . . .
4. worry, I'm worrying, . . .
5. watches, she's watching, . . .
6. writes, he's writing, . . .
7. take, I'm taking, . . .
8. combs, he's combing, . . .
9. gets up, she's getting up, . . .
10. smiles, he's smiling, . . .
11. bark, they're barking, . . .
12. wears, she's wearing, . . .

WORKBOOK PAGE 5

D. What Are They Saying?

1. Do you recommend
2. Does, bake

3. Does, get up
4. Do, complain
5. Does, speak
6. Does, live
7. Do you watch
8. Does she play
9. Does he practice
10. Do you plant
11. Does he add
12. Do you wear
13. Does she ride
14. Does he jog
15. Do we need
16. Does he iron
17. Do they have

WORKBOOK PAGE 6

E. Puzzle

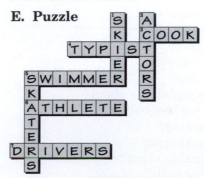

F. What's the Answer?

1. b   5. b
2. c   6. c
3. b   7. a
4. c   8. b

WORKBOOK PAGE 7

G. What Are They Saying?

1. don't, doesn't
   isn't, cook
2. don't, I'm
   drive
3. Do you
   don't, I'm
   You're, type
4. composes, he's
5. isn't, doesn't
   swimmer
6. don't
   speak, speaker

H. Listening

1. he does
2. she isn't
3. they are
4. they do
5. she doesn't
6. it is
7. he isn't
8. I do
9. she doesn't
10. he is
11. I'm not
12. we do
13. she is
14. they aren't
15. we don't

WORKBOOK PAGE 9

J. What's the Question?

1. What are you waiting for?
2. Who is he thinking about?
3. What are they ironing?
4. Who are you calling?
5. Who is she dancing with?
6. What's he watching?
7. What are they complaining about?
8. Who is she playing baseball with?
9. Who are they visiting?
10. What are you looking at?
11. What are you writing about?
12. Who is he arguing with?
13. Who is she knitting a sweater for?
14. What are you making?
15. Who are you sending an e-mail to?
16. What are they worrying about?
17. Who is she talking to?
18. Who is he skating with?

WORKBOOK PAGE 10

K. What Are They Saying?

1. your
   We're, them
2. his
   He, them, his
3. they, me
4. her
   She, them
5. your
   I, my
6. your
   I'm, her
7. They, them
8. us, it
9. he, it
10. your
    She, my

WORKBOOK PAGE 11

L. What's the Word?

1. with
2. —
3. at
4. to
5. about
6. —
7. —, with
8. for
9. —

UNIT 2

WORKBOOK PAGE 12

A. Herbert's Terrible Day!

1. had
2. got up
3. ate
4. rushed
5. ran
6. missed
7. waited
8. decided
9. arrived
10. sat
11. began
12. called
13. typed
14. made
15. fixed
16. finished
17. put
18. spilled
19. went
20. ordered
21. felt
22. forgot
23. crashed
24. fell
25. broke
26. hurt
27. left
28. took
29. went

WORKBOOK PAGE 13

B. Listening

1. every day
2. yesterday
3. every day
4. yesterday
5. every day
6. yesterday
7. yesterday
8. every day
9. yesterday
10. every day
11. every day
12. yesterday

C. What's the Word?

1. wanted
2. lifted
3. painted
4. roller-bladed
5. planted
6. needed
7. waited
8. decided

D. Puzzle: *What Did They Do?*

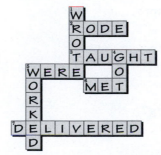

E. What's the Question?

1. Did you buy
2. Did they take
3. Did she see
4. Did he speak
5. Did you break
6. Did it begin
7. Did she fly
8. Did you have
9. Did they go
10. Did I sing
11. Did he meet
12. Did you lose

F. What's the Answer?

1. they were bored
2. I wasn't hungry
3. they were tired
4. she wasn't prepared
5. he was angry
6. I wasn't on time
7. she wasn't thirsty
8. I was scared
9. they were sad

WORKBOOK PAGE 15

G. Something Different

1. didn't drive, drove
2. didn't come, came
3. didn't take, took
4. didn't go, went
5. didn't forget, forgot
6. didn't wear, wore
7. didn't teach, taught
8. didn't eat, ate
9. didn't give, gave
10. didn't sit, sat
11. didn't have, had
12. didn't sing, sang

WORKBOOK PAGES 16–17

H. What Are They Saying?

1. Did you
   didn't, was
2. Did you
   didn't
   met
3. Did
   did
   wasn't
4. Did
   she didn't
   weren't

5. Did, fall
   he didn't
   fell
   was
6. Did
   I didn't, rode
   was
   was
7. Did you
   did, was
   didn't
   was
8. Was
   was, Were
   I wasn't, didn't
9. Did
   did
   didn't
   were
10. Did
    they didn't
    danced
    were
11. did
    I did, bought
    Did you
    didn't
    wasn't
12. were
    were
    I was, was
    was
    wasn't

WORKBOOK PAGE 18

I. How Did It Happen?

1. He sprained his ankle while he was playing tennis.
2. She ripped her pants while she was exercising.
3. I broke my arm while I was playing volleyball.
4. He poked himself in the eye while he was fixing his sink.
5. We hurt ourselves while we were skateboarding.
6. They tripped and fell while they were dancing.
7. He burned himself while he was cooking french fries.
8. She got a black eye while she was fighting with the kid across the street.
9. I cut myself while I was chopping carrots.
10. He lost his cell phone while he was jogging in the park.

L. What's the Question?

1. Who did you meet?
2. What did she lose?
3. Where did you do your exercises?
4. When did they leave?
5. How did she get here?
6. Where did he sing?
7. How long did they stay?
8. What kind of movie did you see?
9. Why did he cry?
10. Who did she write a letter to?
11. What did they complain about?
12. How many grapes did you eat?
13. Where did he speak?
14. How long did they lift weights?
15. Who did she give a present to?
16. What kind of pie did you order?
17. How many videos did you rent?
18. Who did they send an e-mail to?
19. When did he fall asleep?
20. When did you lose your hat?

M. Our Vacation

1. we didn't
   did you go
   We went
2. we didn't
   did you get there
   We got there by plane.
3. it didn't
   did it leave
   It left
4. we didn't
   weather did you have
   We had
5. we didn't
   hotel did you stay in
   We stayed in a small hotel.
6. we didn't
   food did you eat
   We ate Japanese food.
7. we didn't
   did you take (with you)
   We took
8. we didn't
   did you get around the city
   We got around the city by taxi.
9. we didn't
   did you meet
   We met
10. we didn't
    did you buy
    We bought

11. we didn't
    did you speak
    We spoke English.
12. we did
    money did you spend
    We spent . . .

N. Sound It Out!

1. these
2. did
3. Rita
4. big
5. green
6. mittens
7. knit
8. Did Rita knit these big green mittens?
9. Greek
10. his
11. Richard
12. every
13. speaks
14. with
15. week
16. sister
17. Richard speaks Greek with his sister every week.

UNIT 3

A. What Are They Saying?

1. No, I didn't.
   rode
   I'm going to ride
2. No, he didn't.
   wore
   He's going to wear
3. No, she didn't.
   gave
   She's going to give
4. No, they didn't.
   drove
   They're going to drive
5. No, we didn't.
   had
   We're going to have
6. No, I didn't.
   went
   I'm going to go
7. No, he didn't.
   wrote
   He's going to write
8. No, she didn't.
   left
   She's going to leave

WORKBOOK PAGES 25–26

B. Bad Connections!

1. your dentist going to do
2. are you going to go
3. is she going to move to Alaska
4. What are they going to give you?
5. What are you going to do?
6. When are you going to get married?
7. Who are you going to meet?
8. What are you going to name your new puppy?
9. Why are they going to sell your house?
10. Where are you going to go?
11. Who do you have to call?
12. Why are you going to fire me?

C. Listening

1. b
2. a
3. a
4. b
5. a
6. b
7. b
8. a
9. a
10. b
11. b
12. a

WORKBOOK PAGE 27

D. The Pessimist and the Optimists

1. won't have   you will, You'll
2. will hurt   he won't, He won't
3. won't   she will, She'll
4. will be   she won't, She won't
5. won't lose   you will, You'll
6. will forget   they won't, They won't
7. won't fix   he will, He'll
8. won't   they will, They'll like
9. I'll   you won't, You won't

WORKBOOK PAGE 28

E. What Will Be Happening?

1. she will, She'll be doing
2. I will, I'll be filling out
3. he won't, He'll be working out
4. they will, They'll be cleaning
5. he will, He'll be browsing
6. we will, We'll be watching
7. she won't, She'll be attending
8. it won't, It'll be raining

WORKBOOK PAGE 29

G. What Are They Saying?

1. giving, will you be giving
2. will you be doing, be doing
3. talk, talk, studying
4. having/eating, will you be having/eating

WORKBOOK PAGE 31

I. Whose Is It?

1. yours
2. mine
3. his
4. hers
5. theirs
6. ours
7. hers
8. hers

WORKBOOK PAGES 32–33

K. What Does It Mean?

1. b
2. c
3. b
4. b
5. a
6. a
7. c
8. b
9. a
10. c
11. a
12. c
13. a
14. b
15. a
16. b
17. a
18. b
19. c
20. a
21. c
22. a
23. b
24. c

L. Listening: *Looking Forward*

1. a
2. c
3. b
4. b
5. c
6. b
7. b
8. a
9. c

WORKBOOK PAGES 34–35

CHECK-UP TEST: Units 1–3

A.

1. are
   dance
2. drives
3. you're
   swimmers
4. I'm
   typist
5. aren't, skiers

B.

1. didn't, was
   spoke
2. didn't
   bought
3. Did
   didn't, got
4. didn't, taught
   was
5. Did
   didn't, talked
   wasn't

C.

1. What are you writing about?
2. What are they going to fix?
3. Where did he hike?
4. When will she be ready?
5. How did they arrive?
6. How long will you be staying?
7. How many people is she going to hire?

D.

1. She's adjusting her satellite dish.
2. He chats online.
3. I'm going to visit my mother-in-law.
4. They delivered groceries.
5. He was baking a cake.
6. I'll take the bus.
7. We'll be watching TV.
8. I was chopping carrots.

E.

1. I am
2. they won't
3. you did
4. he does
5. she isn't
6. we do
7. she doesn't
8. we will

GAZETTE

WORKBOOK PAGES 35a–d

A. Immigration Around the World

1. d
2. c
3. d
4. a
5. b
6. a
7. c
8. b
9. c
10. a

B. Fact File

1. c
2. d

C. Ellis Island

1. b
2. c
3. b
4. c
5. d
6. a
7. d

D. Interview

1. d
2. a
3. b
4. b
5. a
6. c

E. We've Got Mail! What's the Word?

1. c
2. d
3. b
4. c
5. a
6. b
7. d
8. b

F. We've Got Mail! What's the Sentence?

1. c
2. a
3. d
4. b
5. c
6. d

G. Fun with Idioms!

1. d
2. a
3. c
4. d
5. b
6. a

H. "Can-Do" Review

1. e
2. i
3. a
4. g
5. b
6. j
7. d
8. f
9. c
10. h

UNIT 4

WORKBOOK PAGE 36

A. For Many Years

1. I've ridden
2. I've flown
3. I've given
4. I've spoken
5. I've taken
6. I've done
7. I've drawn
8. I've written
9. I've driven

B. Listening

1. a
2. b
3. a
4. b
5. b
6. a
7. a
8. b

WORKBOOK PAGE 37

C. I've Never

1. I've never flown
2. I've never gotten
3. I've never ridden
4. I've never drawn
5. I've never written
6. I've never taken
7. I've never sung
8. I've never swum
9. I've never been
10. I've never gone
11. I've never given
12. I've never seen

D. Listening

1. Yes
2. No
3. No
4. Yes
5. No
6. Yes
7. No
8. No

WORKBOOK PAGE 38

E. What Are They Saying?

1. Have you ever gotten
   I got
2. Have you ever ridden
   I rode
3. Have you ever worn
   I wore
4. Have you ever gone
   I went
5. Have you ever given
   I gave
6. Have you ever fallen
   I fell

WORKBOOK PAGE 39

G. What Are They Saying?

1. Have, eaten
   they have, They ate
2. Has, driven
   he has, He drove
3. Has, gone
   she has, She went
4. Have, seen
   we have, We saw
5. Have, taken
   they have, They took
6. Have, spoken
   I have, I spoke
7. Have, written
   you have, You wrote
8. Have, met
   we have, We met

WORKBOOK PAGE 40

H. Not Today

1. They've, eaten
   They ate
2. She's, gone
   She went
3. He's, worn
   He wore

4. We've, done
   We did
5. He's, given
   He gave
6. I've, seen
   I saw
7. We've, bought
   We bought
8. She's, visited
   She visited
9. He's, taken
   He took

WORKBOOK PAGE 41

I. What's the Word?

1. go
2. went
3. gone
4. seen
5. saw
6. see
7. ate
8. eaten
9. eat
10. write
11. written
12. wrote
13. wear
14. worn
15. wore
16. spoke
17. speak
18. spoken
19. driven
20. drive
21. drove
22. do
23. did
24. done

WORKBOOK PAGES 42–43

J. What Are They Saying?

1. I've, done
   I did
   have, written
   I have
2. I've, swum
   I swam
3. I've, taken
   I took
   Have, taken
   I have, took
4. He's, gotten
   He got
5. We've, eaten
   We ate
   eaten
6. I've, spoken
   I spoke

WORKBOOK PAGES 44–45

L. In a Long Time

1. I haven't ridden
2. haven't bought
3. I haven't flown
4. I haven't taken
5. I haven't swum
6. hasn't eaten
7. hasn't cleaned

8. He hasn't read
9. I haven't studied
10. haven't seen
11. I haven't given
12. He hasn't made
13. haven't gone
14. I haven't danced

M. Puzzle: *What Have They Already Done?*

WORKBOOK PAGES 46–47

N. A Lot of Things to Do

1. He's already gone to the supermarket.
2. He hasn't cleaned his apartment yet.
3. He's already gotten a haircut.
4. He hasn't baked a cake yet.
5. He's already fixed his CD player.
6. She's already taken a shower.
7. She hasn't done her exercises yet.
8. She hasn't fed the cat yet.
9. She's already walked the dog.
10. She hasn't eaten breakfast yet.
11. They haven't done their laundry yet.
12. They've already gotten their paychecks.
13. They've already paid their bills.
14. They haven't packed their suitcases yet.
15. They haven't said good-bye to their friends yet.
16. She's already written to Mrs. Lane.
17. She's already called Mr. Sanchez.
18. She hasn't met with Ms. Wong yet.
19. She hasn't read her e-mail yet.
20. She's already sent a fax to the Ace Company.

O. Listening

	Yes	No		Yes	No
1.	✔	___	5.	___	✔
	___	✔		___	✔
2.	___	✔	6.	✔	___
	___	✔		✔	___
3.	✔	___	7.	✔	___
	___	✔		✔	___
4.	✔	___	8.	___	✔
	✔	___		✔	___

P. What Are They Saying?

1. have, spoke
   did
   flown
2. Have
   haven't, saw
   see
   seen
3. taken
   took
   Have, sent
   sent
   Have, given
4. Have
   have, went
   Have, gone/been
   have, I went/was
5. did
   gave
   are you going to buy
   spent
   did you
   bought
   listen
6. I'm not, taken
   got
   Have
   I have, ate
   washed/done

WORKBOOK PAGE 50

R. _J_ ulia's Broken Keyboard

1.
Judy,
   Have you seen my blue and _y_ellow
_j_acket at _y_our house? I think I left it there
_y_esterday after the _j_azz concert. I've looked
everywhere, and I _j_ust can't find it anywhere.
   Julia

2.
Dear _J_ennifer,
   We're sorry _y_ou haven't been able to visit
us this _y_ear. Do _y_ou think _y_ou could come
in _J_une or _J_uly? We really en_j_oyed _y_our visit
last _y_ear. We really want to see _y_ou again.
   Julia

3.
_J_eff,
   _J_ack and I have gone out _j_ogging, but we'll
be back in _j_ust a few minutes. Make _y_ourself
comfortable. _Y_ou can wait for us in the _y_ard.
We haven't eaten lunch _y_et. We'll have some
_y_ogurt and orange _j_uice when we get back.
   Julia

4.
Dear _J_ane,
   We _j_ust received the beautiful pa_j_amas _y_ou
sent to _J_immy. Thank _y_ou very much.
_J_immy is too _y_oung to write to _y_ou himself,
but he says "Thank _y_ou." He's already worn
the pa_j_amas, and he's en_j_oying them a lot.
   Julia

5.
Dear _J_anet,
   _J_ack and I are coming to visit _y_ou and
_J_ohn in New _Y_ork. We've been to New _Y_ork
before, but we haven't visited the Statue of
Liberty or the Empire State Building _y_et.
See _y_ou in _J_anuary or maybe in _J_une.
   Julia

6.
Dear _J_oe,
   We got a letter from _J_ames last week.
He has en_j_oyed college a lot this _y_ear. His
favorite sub_j_ects are German and _J_apanese.
He's looking for a _j_ob as a _j_ournalist in
_J_apan, but he hasn't found one yet.
   Julia

WORKBOOK PAGE 51

S. _Is_ or _Has_?

1. has		11. is	
2. is		12. has	
3. is		13. is	
4. has		14. has	
5. is		15. has	
6. is		16. is	
7. has		17. has	
8. is		18. is	
9. is		19. is	
10. has		20. has	

UNIT 5

WORKBOOK PAGE 52

A. How Long?

1. I've had a headache since
2. They've been married for
3. He's owned a motorcycle since
4. She's been interested in astronomy for
5. I've had a cell phone since
6. We've known each other since
7. They've had a dog for
8. I've had problems with my upstairs neighbor for
9. She's been a computer programmer since
10. He's played in the school orchestra since
11. There have been mice in our attic for

WORKBOOK PAGE 53

B. What's the Question?

1. How long has, wanted to be an engineer
2. How long has, owned his own house
3. How long have, been married
4. How long have, been interested in photography
5. How long has, worn glasses
6. How long have, known how to snowboard
7. How long has, had a girlfriend
8. How long has, been a pizza shop in town

WORKBOOK PAGE 55

D. Since When?

1. I'm
   I've been sick
2. has
   She's had
3. knows
   He's known
4. They're
   They've been
5. We're
   We've been
6. have
   I've had
7. It's
   It's been
8. plays
   She's
9. is
   He's been
10. I'm
    I've been

WORKBOOK PAGE 56

E. Listening

1. b	4. b	7. a	10. a
2. b	5. a	8. b	11. b
3. a	6. a	9. b	12. a

F. Crossword

WORKBOOK PAGE 57

G. Scrambled Sentences

1. Julie has liked jazz since she was a teenager.
2. He's known how to play the piano since he was a little boy.

3. I've been interested in astronomy since I was young.
4. They've been engaged since they finished college.
5. He's been a chef since he graduated from cooking school.
6. She's wanted to be a teacher since she was eighteen years old.
7. They've owned their own business since they moved here a year ago.

WORKBOOK PAGE 58

I. Then and Now

1. walk
   They've walked
   they
   walked
2. speaks
   He's spoken
   he spoke
3. is
   She's been
   she was
4. taught
   he teaches
   He's taught
5. has
   visited
   visited
   visit
6. has
   She's had
   had

WORKBOOK PAGE 59

J. Looking Back

1. has Victor been
   He's been a musician, 1990
2. was he
   He was a photographer, 7 years
3. has Mrs. Sanchez taught
   She's taught science, 1995
4. did she teach
   She taught math, 9 years
5. did your grandparents have
   They had a cat, 11 years
6. have they had
   They've had a dog, 1998
7. has Betty worked
   She's worked at the bank, 2000
8. did she work
   She worked at the mall, 2 years
9. did your parents live
   They lived in New York, 20 years
10. have they lived
    They've lived in Miami, 2001

L. Listening

1. b	4. b	7. b	10. b
2. b	5. b	8. a	11. b
3. a	6. a	9. b	12. a

GAZETTE

WORKBOOK PAGES 61a–d

A. "24/7"

1. a	4. d	7. c	10. b
2. c	5. b	8. d	
3. b	6. a	9. d	

B. Fact File

1. a   2. c

C. Interview

1. c	3. b	5. d	7. c
2. a	4. c	6. b	8. d

E. Fun with Idioms: What's the Expression?

1. chicken	4. the top banana
2. a couch potato	5. a real peach
3. a real ham	6. a smart cookie

F. Fun with Idioms: Crossword

H. We've Got Mail!

1. c	4. d	7. b	10. c
2. d	5. c	8. a	11. a
3. b	6. a	9. d	12. b

I. "Can-Do" Review

1. h	4. a	7. b	10. e
2. d	5. f	8. i	
3. j	6. c	9. g	

UNIT 6

WORKBOOK PAGE 62

A. What's the Word?

1. since	4. since	7. since
2. for	5. since	8. for
3. for	6. for	

B. Choose

1. a	3. b	5. b
2. b	4. a	6. b

WORKBOOK PAGE 63

C. How Long?

1. I've been studying since
2. She's been feeling sick for
3. He's been having problems with his car for
4. They've been arguing since
5. We've been waiting for
6. It's been ringing since
7. He's been talking for
8. They've been dating since
9. I've been teaching since
10. You've been chatting online for

WORKBOOK PAGE 64

D. What Are They Doing?

1. is looking
   He's been looking
2. is jogging
   She's been jogging
3. is barking
   It's been barking
4. are planting
   They've been planting
5. is doing
   He's been doing
6. is browsing
   She's been browsing
7. are assembling
   They've been assembling
8. baking
   I've been baking
9. are making
   You've been making

E. Listening

1. a	4. b	6. a	8. a
2. b	5. b	7. b	9. b
3. a			

G. What Are They Saying?

1. Have you been waiting
   have
   I've been waiting
2. Has it been snowing
   it has
   It's been snowing
3. Has he been taking
   he has
   He's been taking
4. Have you been working
   I haven't
   been working
5. Has, been making
   it has
   It's been making
6. Have you been vacuuming
   I have
   I've been vacuuming
7. Have they been studying
   they have
   They've been studying
8. Have we been running
   have
   We've been running
9. Have you been wearing
   I haven't
   I've been wearing
10. Have you been playing
    I haven't
    I've been playing

H. Listening

1. a	5. b	9. b	13. b
2. b	6. b	10. a	14. a
3. b	7. a	11. b	15. b
4. a	8. a	12. a	

I. Sound It Out!

1. interested
2. is
3. Steve's
4. in
5. history
6. sister
7. very
8. Chinese
9. Steve's sister is very interested in Chinese history.
10. receive
11. this

12. any
13. Peter
14. week
15. didn't
16. e-mail
17. Peter didn't receive any e-mail this week.

K. What's Happening?

1. We've been eating
   We've, eaten
   We haven't eaten
2. She's been seeing
   She's, see
   She hasn't seen
3. He's been swimming
   He's, swum
4. She's been going
   She's, gone
5. He's been talking
   He's, talked
   he hasn't talked
6. They've been writing
   They've, written
   they haven't written
7. he's been making
   He's, made
   He hasn't made
8. She's been studying
   She's, studied
   she hasn't studied
9. He's been reading
   He's, read
   he hasn't read
10. They've been
    complaining
    They've, complained
    haven't complained

L. Listening

1. a	4. a	7. b	10. b
2. b	5. a	8. a	11. a
3. b	6. b	9. b	12. b

M. Which Word?

1. leaking	7. given
2. flying	8. taken
3. run	9. gone
4. made	10. has been ringing
5. have you been	11. singing
6. see	

O. A New Life

1. He's never lived in a big city
2. He's never taken English lessons
3. He's never taken the subway
4. He's never shopped in American supermarkets
5. He's never eaten American food
6. He's never played American football

8. They've been living in a big city
9. They've been taking English lessons
10. They've been taking the subway
11. They've been shopping in American supermarkets
12. They've been eating American food
13. They've been playing American football

WORKBOOK PAGES 76–77

CHECK-UP TEST: Units 4–6

A.

1. have, eaten
2. hasn't taken
3. haven't written
4. has, gone
5. haven't paid
6. has, had

B.

1. Have you spoken
2. Has he ridden
3. Have they gotten
4. Has he, flown
5. Has she, been
6. Have you met

C.

1. It's been sunny
2. We've been browsing
3. She's had
4. He's been studying
5. They've been arguing
6. I've known
7. She's been
8. We've been cleaning

D.

1. She's been working at the bank since
2. They've been barking for
3. It's been snowing for
4. I've wanted to be an astronaut since

E.

1. He's owned
   he owned
2. I've been
   I was
3. She's liked
   she liked

F.

1. b
2. a
3. b
4. a
5. a
6. b

UNIT 7

WORKBOOK PAGE 78

A. What Do They { Enjoy Doing / Like to Do }?

1. enjoy
2. likes to, Talking
3. enjoy
4. like to, Knitting
5. enjoy
6. likes to, delivering
7. enjoy, being
8. likes to, planting
9. enjoys, chatting
10. like to, playing
11. enjoy
12. likes to, going
13. enjoy

WORKBOOK PAGE 80

C. What's the Word?

1. complain
2. sitting
3. eat
4. clean
5. wear
6. cleaning
7. go
8. going
9. sit
10. complaining
11. eating
12. wearing

WORKBOOK PAGE 82

F. My Energetic Grandfather

1. to play/playing
2. to play
3. play

WORKBOOK PAGE 83

H. Choose

1. to buy
2. moving
3. going
4. changing
5. get
6. retiring

WORKBOOK PAGE 85

K. What's the Word?

1. rearranging
2. eating
3. worrying
4. to get/getting
5. to exercise/exercising
6. to ask/asking
7. arguing
8. to take/taking
9. paying, to pay/paying
10. to fall/falling

L. Good Decisions

1. biting
2. to do/doing
3. to cook
4. to cook/cooking
5. paying
6. cleaning
7. gossiping
8. interrupting

M. Problems!

1. falling
   falling
2. to lift/lifting
   to lift/lifting
   lifting
3. to tease/teasing
   teasing
   crying
   teasing
4. driving
   to drive/driving
   to drive/driving
5. dressing
   to dress/dressing
   dressing
6. stepping
   to dance/dancing
   going

WORKBOOK PAGE 87

N. Listening

1. a	5. a	9. a	13. a
2. a	6. a	10. b	14. a
3. b	7. b	11. b	15. b
4. b	8. b	12. b	

O. What Does It Mean?

1. b	4. b	7. b	10. b
2. c	5. c	8. a	11. b
3. a	6. a	9. c	12. c

UNIT 8

WORKBOOK PAGE 88

A. Before

1. had eaten
2. had, gotten
3. had, visited
4. had driven
5. had, cut
6. had spent
7. had, gone
8. had made
9. had seen
10. had, left
11. had had
12. had, given
13. had lost

WORKBOOK PAGE 90

C. Late for Everything

1. had, left
2. had, begun
3. had, gone---
4. had, closed
5. had, started
6. had, left
7. had, arrived

WORKBOOK PAGE 91

D. In a Long Time

1. hadn't listened
2. hadn't seen
3. hadn't had
4. hadn't gone
5. hadn't remembered
6. hadn't ironed, hadn't shaved
7. hadn't lost
8. hadn't skied
9. hadn't gotten
10. hadn't taken off
11. hadn't studied
12. hadn't ridden

WORKBOOK PAGES 92–93

E. Working Hard

1. She was studying for her science test.
2. She had already written an English composition.
3. She hadn't practiced the trombone yet.
4. She hadn't read the next history chapter yet.
5. She hadn't memorized her lines for the school play yet.
6. He was hooking up the new printer.
7. He had already sent an e-mail to the boss.
8. He had already given the employees their paychecks.
9. He hadn't written to the Bentley Company yet.
10. He hadn't taken two packages to the post office yet.
11. They were cleaning the garage.
12. They had already assembled Billy's new bicycle.
13. They had already fixed the fence.
14. They hadn't repaired the roof yet.
15. They hadn't started to build a tree house yet.
16. She was playing squash.
17. She had already done yoga.
18. She had already gone jogging.
19. She hadn't lifted weights yet.
20. She hadn't swum across the pool 10 times yet.

WORKBOOK PAGE 94

F. What Had They Been Doing?

1. had been talking
2. had been living
3. had been working
4. had been going out
5. had been planning

(continued)

6. had been thinking about
7. had been getting
8. had been borrowing
9. had been eating
10. had been rehearsing
11. had been looking forward
12. had been training
13. had been arriving

WORKBOOK PAGE 96

I. Marylou's Broken Keyboard

1.

> Roger,
>
> I'm afraid there's something wrong with the fireplace in the living room. Also, the refrigerator is broken. I've been calling the landlord for three days on his cell phone, but he hasn't called back. I hope he calls me tomorrow.
>
> Marylou

2.

> Louise,
>
> I'm terribly worried about my brother Larry's health. He hurt his leg while he was playing baseball. He had already dislocated his shoulder while he was surfing last Friday. According to his doctor, he is also having problems with his blood pressure and with his right wrist. He really should try to relax and take life a little easier.
>
> Marylou

3.

> Arnold,
>
> Can you possibly recommend a good restaurant in your neighborhood? I'm planning on taking my relatives to lunch tomorrow, but I'm not sure where.
>
> We ate at a very nice Greek restaurant near your apartment building last month, but I haven't been able to remember the name. Do you know the place?
>
> Your friend,
> Marylou

4.

> Rosa,
>
> I have been planning a trip to Florida. I'll be flying to Orlando on Friday, and I'll be returning three days later. Have you ever been there? I remember you had family members who lived in Florida several years ago.
>
> Please write back.
>
> All my love,
> Marylou

WORKBOOK PAGE 97

J. Listening

1. c	7. a	13. b	19. b
2. b	8. b	14. a	20. a
3. c	9. c	15. c	21. b
4. b	10. b	16. c	22. c
5. c	11. a	17. b	23. a
6. b	12. c	18. c	24. c

WORKBOOK PAGES 98–99

CHECK-UP TEST: Units 7–8

A.

1. eating	5. Swimming
2. wrestling	6. to skate
3. to stop	7. talking
4. boxing	8. doing

B.

1. hadn't spoken
2. had, done
3. had, left
4. hadn't written
5. hadn't had
6. hadn't taken
7. hadn't eaten
8. hadn't gone

C.

1. had been working
2. had been training
3. had been arguing
4. had been planning

D.

1. b	4. b
2. a	5. a
3. b	

GAZETTE

WORKBOOK PAGES 99a–d

A. The Jamaican Bobsled Team

1. b	4. a	7. c	10. a
2. a	5. b	8. b	
3. c	6. d	9. d	

B. Fact File

1. b	2. d

C. Interview

1. d	4. d	7. a	10. a
2. c	5. b	8. c	
3. b	6. d	9. b	

E. Fun with Idioms: What's the Meaning?

1. leg   Good luck!
2. back   Don't bother me!
3. tongue   Be quiet!
4. chin   Don't be sad!
5. foot   Try hard!
6. eye   Pay attention!

F. Fun with Idioms: Finish the Conversations

1. Keep your eye on the ball
2. Hold your tongue!
3. Keep your chin up!
4. Get off my back
5. Break a leg!
6. Put your best foot forward!

G. We've Got Mail!

1. c	4. d	7. b	10. c
2. d	5. c	8. b	
3. b	6. a	9. d	

H. "Can-Do" Review

1. g	4. a	7. j	10. b
2. d	5. h	8. f	
3. i	6. c	9. e	

UNIT 9

WORKBOOK PAGE 100

A. What Are They Saying?

1. pick him up
2. turned it on
3. take them back
4. fill them out
5. hang it up
6. hook it up
7. throw them out
8. took it back
9. took them down
10. call her up

WORKBOOK PAGE 101

B. What Are They Saying?

1. turn on
   turn it on
2. hand, in
   hand it in
3. wake up
   wake them up
4. turn, off
   turn it off
5. take off
   take them off
6. put, away
   put them away

7. Put, on
   put them on
8. bring, back
   bring her back

WORKBOOK PAGE 103

D. What Are They Saying?

1. do it over
2. gave it back
3. hook it up
4. think it over
5. look it up
6. turn him down
7. throw them away
8. written it down
9. cross them out
10. turned it off

WORKBOOK PAGE 104

E. What's the Word?

1. put away
2. hook up
3. take back
4. wake up
5. call up
6. write down
7. clean up
8. put away
9. throw out
10. hang up

WORKBOOK PAGE 105

F. What Should They Do?

1. think it over
2. give it back
3. used it up
4. look it up
5. figure it out
6. wake them up
7. turn it off
8. throw them out

G. Listening

1. b	4. b	6. a	8. a
2. b	5. b	7. b	9. b
3. a			

WORKBOOK PAGE 106

H. Come Up With the Right Answer

1. take after
   take after him
2. heard from
   hear from him
3. called on
   call on me

(continued)

4. looking through
   looked through them
5. got over
   got over it
6. look up to
   look up to me
7. ran into
   ran into her
8. get along with
   get along with her
9. picks on
   picks on them

WORKBOOK PAGE 107

J. Choose

1. b   5. a   9. a   13. b
2. a   6. b   10. b   14. b
3. b   7. b   11. a
4. b   8. a   12. a

WORKBOOK PAGE 108

K. What Does It Mean?

1. b   3. b   5. a   7. b
2. c   4. c   6. a   8. c

L. Listening

1. c   4. a   7. a   10. b
2. b   5. b   8. c   11. a
3. c   6. c   9. c   12. b

UNIT 10

WORKBOOK PAGE 109

A. Not the Only One

1. did I   8. I have
2. I do   9. I did
3. can I   10. will I
4. I am   11. do I
5. I will
6. was I
7. am I

WORKBOOK PAGE 110

B. What a Coincidence!

1. do I   7. I was
2. I do   8. I did
3. I did   9. I am
4. have I   10. do I
5. I will   11. am I
6. did I

WORKBOOK PAGE 111

C. Not the Only One

1. did I   7. I can't
2. I'm not   8. am I
3. was I   9. I didn't
4. I can't   10. do I
5. I won't   11. will I
6. have I

WORKBOOK PAGE 112

D. Listening

1. did I   9. do I
2. I am   10. have I
3. will I   11. I'm not
4. I haven't   12. I should
5. I can   13. can I
6. I do   14. do I
7. am I   15. I won't
8. I did

WORKBOOK PAGE 113

G. What Are They Saying?

1. did he   6. they were
2. will she   7. so can
3. he was   8. did he
4. has she   9. I do
5. you should   10. . . ., so has

WORKBOOK PAGE 114

H. What Are They Saying?

1. can I   6. she hasn't
2. they didn't 7. will they
3. is he   8. aren't either
4. she doesn't 9. neither has
5. were they   10. she hadn't

WORKBOOK PAGE 115

I. What Are They Saying?

1. so did she
   she did, too
2. neither could he
   he couldn't either
3. so does he
   he does, too
4. neither does she
   she doesn't either
5. neither had she
   she hadn't either
6. so is he
   he is, too

J. Our Family

1. aren't, been
2. is, playing, doing
3. can, drawing, was
4. doesn't, going
5. isn't, has been taking
6. haven't, lived, for, lived
7. doesn't, hasn't spoken
8. won't, hasn't
9. does, sung, since
10. aren't, up, away
11. doesn't, for
12. aren't, skating, had, skated

WORKBOOK PAGE 117

K. Listening

1. didn't
2. isn't
3. won't
4. have
5. can't
6. doesn't
7. haven't
8. didn't
9. will
10. wasn't
11. is
12. didn't
13. can
14. don't
15. will
16. is
17. have
18. was

WORKBOOK PAGE 118

M. Sound It Out!

1. cooks
2. too
3. shouldn't
4. put
5. cookies
6. good
7. sugar
8. Good cooks shouldn't put too much sugar in their cookies.
9. two
10. books
11. bookcase
12. who
13. took
14. afternoon
15. Susan's
16. Who took two books from Susan's bookcase this afternoon?

WORKBOOK PAGE 119

N. What Does It Mean?

1. j
2. c
3. q
4. s
5. n
6. h
7. i
8. x
9. m
10. v
11. w
12. y
13. b
14. a
15. u
16. l
17. p
18. e
19. o
20. k
21. f
22. t
23. z
24. g
25. d
26. r

WORKBOOK PAGES 120–121

CHECK-UP TEST: Units 9–10

A.

1. it in
2. up to him
3. from her
4. it over
5. it up
6. out of it
7. for it
8. them up
9. them out
10. it down
11. over it

B.

1. so is
2. neither will
3. were, too
4. can't either
5. so have
6. did, too
7. neither has
8. so do
9. neither is

C.

1. isn't
2. will
3. doesn't
4. has
5. didn't

GAZETTE

WORKBOOK PAGES 121a–c

A. From Matchmakers to Dating Services

1. b
2. a
3. c
4. d
5. c
6. b
7. d
8. a
9. c
10. b

B. Fact File

1. c
2. d

C. Around the World

1. c
2. b
3. d
4. b
5. c
6. a
7. d
8. b
9. c
10. d

D. Interview

1. c
2. d
3. b
4. c

E. Fun with Idioms

1. b
2. d
3. c
4. a

F. We've Got Mail!

1. d
2. c
3. a
4. c
5. b
6. d

G. "Can-Do" Review

1. f
2. h
3. a
4. j
5. d
6. b
7. i
8. g
9. c
10. e

UNIT 1: Workbook Pages 123–124

A. Personal Information

1. c	3. a	5. b	7. e
2. f	4. d	6. g	

C. Preventing Identity Theft

1. N	3. Y	5. Y
2. N	4. N	6. N

D. Three Branches of Government

1. legislative
2. Senate
3. Congress
4. makes
5. declare
6. Senators
7. representatives
8. executive
9. enforces
10. President
11. Commander
12. armed forces
13. Cabinet
14. signs
15. law
16. Vice President
17. judicial
18. interprets
19. Supreme Court
20. appoint

UNIT 2: Workbook Pages 125–126

A. Apologizing for Lateness at Work

1. e	3. b	5. a
2. c	4. f	6. d

C. U.S. History 1

1. England
2. Thomas Jefferson
3. John Hancock
4. Constitution
5. Philadelphia
6. Declaration of Independence

D. U.S. History 2

1. Colonial
2. Revolutionary War
3. Constitution
4. President
5. father
6. Civil War

7. South
8. North

E. U.S. History 3: *Timeline*

1. f	3. a	5. b
2. d	4. c	6. e

UNIT 3: Workbook Pages 127–128

A. Calling in Sick at Work

6
4
1
7
5
3
2

B. Calling School to Report a Child's Absence

1. attendance
2. tone
3. name
4. reason
5. This
6. won't
7. sore
8. fever

C. A Note to the Teacher

1. September 29
2. Dear
3. absent
4. school
5. appointment
6. attendance
7. homework
8. Sincerely

D. A Campus Map

1. Tate Theater
2. Parking Lot
3. Garcia Science Center
4. Fifth
5. Tyler Library
6. 5
7. 9
8. 1
9. 7
10. Elm Street

UNIT 4: Workbook Pages 129–130

A. Employment Application Vocabulary

1. e   3. b   5. a   7. c
2. g   4. f   6. d

B. Applying for a Job

1. position, skills
2. apply for, application, complete
3. references
4. current
5. former
6. education history
7. dates of employment

UNIT 5: Workbook Pages 131–133

A. Describing Employment History

1. now
2. long
3. since
4. before
5. did
6. for
7. terminated
8. means
9. job
10. understand
11. incarcerated

B. A Cover Letter and Resume

1. F   3. F   5. T   7. T
2. T   4. F   6. F   8. F

E. An Employee Manual

1. F   4. T   7. F   10. F
2. F   5. F   8. F
3. F   6. T   9. T

UNIT 6: Workbook Pages 134–137

A. Lease Vocabulary

1. f   3. c   5. b
2. d   4. a   6. e

B. Paying Bills

MONEY ORDER

Serial Number	Month–Day–Year	Post Office	U.S. Dollars and Cents
02978251423	11-09-20	90020	$89.91

Amount: EIGHTY-NINE & 91 ###############

PAY TO: California Power and Light   NEGOTIABLE ONLY IN THE U.S.

ADDRESS: P.O. Box 3566

FROM: (student's name printed)   CLERK: 017

Los Angeles, CA 90016

ADDRESS: (student's address)

:00030453 2: 02978251423

C. Bank Forms

NATIONAL FIRST BANK   WITHDRAWAL
Date (date filled in)
ACCOUNT NUMBER   4 0 2 7 4 9 6 3 5
Name (Print) (student's name printed)
Signature (student's signature)   Total $ 50.00
:311098 79:

NATIONAL FIRST BANK
DATE (date filled in)
(student's signature)
SIGN HERE FOR CASH RECEIVED
CASH — 40.00
LIST CHECKS SINGLY 125.00
25.00
TOTAL FROM OTHER SIDE
TOTAL — 190.00
LESS CASH RECEIVED
NET DEPOSIT $ 190.00
:9129 8027 988586519 30937 3820000 108

NATIONAL FIRST BANK
DATE (date filled in)
(student's signature)
SIGN HERE FOR CASH RECEIVED
CASH —
LIST CHECKS SINGLY 200.00
140.00
TOTAL FROM OTHER SIDE
TOTAL — 340.00
LESS CASH RECEIVED 100.00
NET DEPOSIT $ 240.00
:9129 8027 988586519 30937 3820000 108

D. Balancing a Checkbook

151
DATE (date filled in) 20
PAY TO THE ORDER OF Northwest Power $ $43.15
Forty-three and 15/100 ___ Dollars
Memo 210 2423   (student's signature)
:233157221O: 2 2915387 151

152
DATE (date filled in) 20
PAY TO THE ORDER OF Com-Phone $ $51.20
Fifty-one and 20/100 ___ Dollars
Memo 1223134   (student's signature)
:233157221O: 2 2915387 152

153
DATE (date filled in) 20
PAY TO THE ORDER OF Viewcast Cable $ $78.90
Seventy-eight and 90/100 ___ Dollars
Memo 76089335   (student's signature)
:233157221O: 2 2915387 153

(continued)

Number	Date	Transaction	Debit	Credit	Balance
150	4/5/20	Water Company	41.50		899.50
151		Northwest Power	43.15		856.35
152		Com-Phone	51.20		805.15
153		Viewcast Cable	78.90		726.25

E. A Rental Apartment Acceptance Form

Apartment Acceptance Form

Name _____   Date _____

Address _____   Apt. # _____

	NOTE PROBLEMS BELOW	Acceptable?	
		Yes	No
Walls & Ceilings	Bedroom ceiling. Living room wall.		✔
Floors	Living room floor.		✔
Electrical Fixtures	Living room light.		✔
Plumbing Fixtures	The toilet is broken.		✔
Other	Bedroom doorknob.		✔

This form must be returned to the rental office within five days of moving into the apartment.

_____   _____
APARTMENT MANAGER   TENANT
signature

F. Reading the Yellow Pages

1. (254) 298-9911
2. (254) 889-6162
3. (254) 536-9121
4. (254) 536-2113
5. (254) 889-7745

UNIT 7: Workbook Pages 138–140

A. Requests at Work

1. lend, happy
2. lending, welcome

3. please, tables
4. borrow, Thanks
5. copying
6. hang

B. Workplace Notes

3
2
1

2
3
1

C. W-4 Form

1. Yes
2. No
3. One
4. $100,000; $119,000

D. Reading a Paycheck and Pay Stub

1. $12.00 per hour
2. 40
3. 5
4. $570.00
5. $129.00
6. $441.00
7. $5,130.00
8. $1,161.00
9. $3,969.00

UNIT 8: Workbook Pages 141–143

A. Scheduling Medical Appointments

1. make
2. confirm
3. cancel, reschedule

B. Internal Organs

1. lungs
2. heart
3. liver
4. gall bladder
5. stomach
6. intestine
7. colon

D. Immunizations

	at birth	2 months	4 months	6 months	12 months	15 months	18 months	2–3 years	4–6 years
Hepatitis B	✔	✔				✔			
Diphtheria, Tetanus, Pertussis (DTaP)		✔	✔	✔			✔		✔
Polio		✔	✔			✔			✔
Measles, Mumps, Rubella (MMR)						✔			✔
Varicella (Chicken Pox)						✔			✔

E. Recipes and Nutrition

1. tomatoes, celery, potatoes, carrots
2. chicken
3. skim milk

F. Recipe Measurements

1 cup of skim milk

1 pint of water

 2 medium onions

1 tablespoon salt

 1 teaspoon black pepper

 6 tomatoes, chopped

 ½ cup celery, chopped

 3 cups medium potatoes, peeled and chopped

 1 cup carrots, chopped

UNIT 9: Workbook Pages 144–145

A. Returning a Defective Product

1. return
2. matter
3. missing
4. stained
5. exchange
6. refund
7. receipt

B. Sale Prices

1. $120
2. $135
3. $54
4. $29.99
5. $110
6. $30
7. $20
8. $112

C. Supermarket Coupon Math

1. $3.24
2. 1/31/20
3. $2.25
4. $3.75
5. Yes
6. $6.50
7. $1.25

UNIT 10: Workbook Pages 146–147

(Student answers will vary.)

Correlation Key

Student Book Pages	Activity Workbook Pages	Student Book Pages	Activity Workbook Pages
Chapter 1		**Chapter 7**	
2	2–3	82	78–79
3	4–5	84	80–81
4	6–8	86–87	82
7–8	9–11	88–89	83–84
10a	123	90–91	85–87
10b–d	124	94a	138 Exercise A
Chapter 2		94b	138 Exercise B
12	12–13	94c–d	139–140
13	14–17	**Chapter 8**	
14–15	18–19	96–97	88–89
18–19	20–23	100	90
20a–b	125	101	91
20c–f	126	104–105	92–93
Chapter 3		106–107	94–96
22–23	24–26	109	97
25	27	110a	141 Exercise A
26	28–29	110b–c	141–142 Exercises B–C
27	30	110d	143 Exercise D
28–29	31–33	110e–f	143 Exercise E
32a–b	127	Check-Up Test	98–99
32c–d	128	Gazette	99a–d
Check-Up Test	34–35	**Chapter 9**	
Gazette	35a–d	116	100
Chapter 4		117	101–102
38	36	119	103
39	37	122–123	104–105
40	38	124	106–107
41	39	126–127	108
42–43	40–43	130a	144 Exercise A
45	44–45	130b	144 Exercise B
46	46–47	130c–d	145
48	48–50	**Chapter 10**	
50	51	132	109–110
50a–d	129–130	133	111–112
Chapter 5		134–135	113
52–53	52–54	138–139	114–115
56–57	55–57	141	116–117
58–59	58–59	143	118–119
62–63	60–61	144b–c	146
64a	131 Exercise A	144d–f	147
64b	131–133 Exercises B–D	Check-Up Test	120–121
64c–d	133 Exercise E	Gazette	121a–c
Gazette	61a–d		
Chapter 6			
70–71	62–65		
72	66–68		
74–75	69–71		
76–77	72–75		
80a	134 Exercise A		
80b–c	134–136 Exercises B–D		
80d	137 Exercise E		
80e–f	137 Exercise F		
Check-Up Test	76–77		

SIDE by SIDE Plus Activity Workbook Audio Program

The *Side by Side Plus* Activity Workbook Digital Audio CDs contain all Workbook listening activities and GrammarRaps for entertaining language practice through rhythm and music. Students can use the Audio Program to extend their language learning through self-study outside the classroom. The Digital Audio CDs also include MP3 files of the audio program for downloading to a computer or audio player.

Audio Program Contents